ABOUT THE AUTHOR

Darryl W Bullock is a feature writer and publisher who
has worked for a variety of local, national and international publications. Since 2007 he has edited the popular
blog The World's Worst Records (www.worldsworst-
records.co.uk) and in 2013 he published his first book,
The World's Worst Records Volume One. He lives in Bristol
with Henry the dog, twin cats Nell and Ruby, and his
very patient husband.

FLORENCE FOSTER JENKINS

The True Story of the World's Worst Singer

Darryl W. Bullock

Duckworth Overlook

First published in the UK and the US in 2016 by
Duckworth Overlook

LONDON
30 Calvin Street, London E1 6NW
T: 020 7490 7300
E: info@duckworth-publishers.co.uk
www.ducknet.co.uk
For bulk and special sales please contact
sales@duckworth-publishers.co.uk, or write to us at the above address.

A catalogue record for this book is available from the British Library.

ISBN:
UK: 978–0–71565106–3
Typeset by Ian Bahrami

Printed and bound in Great Britain

FLORENCE FOSTER JENKINS

An Appreciation

Florence Foster Jenkins, An Appreciation was issued by the
Melotone Recording Company in 1946, and given away free
with copies of her records.

Contents

Contents

List of Illustrations

All images come from the author's collection, with the exception of that on p. 47, which is reproduced by courtesy of the Billy Rose Theatre Division, New York Public Library. 'Publicity photograph of St. Clair Bayfield', New York Public Library Digital Collections 1900–1910.

Note on Sources

All direct quotes attributed to Gregor Benko, Donald Collup, Richard Connema, Mark McMunn, Peter Quilter, Nancy Schimmel and Stephen Temperley are from interviews conducted by the author.

All direct quotes attributed to Cosme McMoon come from the RCA audio recording *Chick Crumpacker Interviews Cosme McMoon*, issued in 1954 to promote the release of *A Florence! Foster!! Jenkins!!! Recital!!!!*.

All direct quotes from Kathleen 'Kay' Bayfield and Florence Darnault are taken from a conversation recorded by Bruce Hungerford in 1970, known as the Hungerford Tape, currently in the Hungerford Collection of the International Piano Archives, University of Maryland.

Overture

On 25 October 1944 a monumental event in the world of music took place. It may not have had the immediate impact of Elvis Presley's first TV appearance, or of the Beatles' debut on the Ed Sullivan Show, or of Bob Dylan plugging in his electric guitar, but on that night, from the hallowed stage of Carnegie Hall (where, two decades later, both Dylan and the Beatles would appear), a concert was given that – like those other magical musical moments – people are still discussing to this day. And now, more than seventy years after her death, the woman who stood on that stage that night is finally about to become a star. Routinely cited as the worst opera singer of all time, until now Narcissa Florence Foster, who found infamy under her married name as Florence Foster Jenkins, has been venerated by a select band of admirers as a camp, kitsch legend – 'the tone-dumb darling of the tone-deaf', as critic Irving Johnson put it.[1] Thanks to Meryl Streep, who portrays the discordant diva in Stephen Frears' movie of her life, she is on the cusp of being discovered by a whole new audience.

The world of opera has presented us with a wealth of extraordinary singers, whose flames have burned

bright and who have cast great shadows over their contemporaries, yet there never has been a soprano who
has come close to eclipsing the fame of the legendary
Florence Foster Jenkins – although the shortcomings
of the woman who preferred to be known as Madame
Jenkins, and who signed herself Lady Florence, were
nothing short of breathtaking. She possessed, as David
Bowie once said, 'the worst set of pipes in the world
of music'.[2] Even though this dumpy septuagenarian
couldn't carry a tune in a bucket (*Newsweek* magazine
said that her voice 'rocked like a drunken sailor in a
gale' and that she 'would have been more at home in
a fish market than in a fashionable ballroom';[3] Robert
Rushmore, author of *The Singing Voice*, wrote that she
'sang like ten million pigs to the delight of her screaming fans'[4]), the matronly musician stubbornly squawked
her way through her material, along the way earning
herself the soubriquet 'The First Lady of the Sliding
Scale'. Styling herself a coloratura soprano (an opera
singer who specialises in music that features lively runs
and other high-register vocal gymnastics), she cheer-
fully attacked material, such as Mozart's notoriously
demanding *Queen of the Night* aria, that would have
taxed even the most accomplished singers and, accompanied by her long-suffering pianist Cosme McMoon,
treated her besotted audience to what *Life* magazine
described as 'a series of gargles and hoots that had to be
heard to be believed'.

It's no surprise that her performances are often viewed as a tragic burlesque, nor that some critics insisted that she knew perfectly well how bad she was, that she lapped up the infamy and consequently laughed all the way to the bank. Those who knew her, however, were adamant that she was absolutely sincere in her conviction that she was truly gifted, and that this dizzy diva was innocently unaware of her distinct lack of talent. 'In that strange realm far at the back of her mind and nearly beyond the reach of her conscious awareness, Florence Foster Jenkins sang with a purity and a soaring brilliance which outshone all the coloraturas of all ages and all lands,' wrote Milton Bendiner a couple of years after her death. 'Her savoir-faire was an innocent and wholly spontaneous travesty of the art of song. Madame Jenkins devoted herself whole heartedly to her exalted, though eccentric, calling.'[5] *New York* magazine was less effusive, labelling her 'charmingly deranged'.[6]

Her story is one of triumph in the face of adversity, of courage and conviction, and above all of the belief that with dedication and commitment (and a whole lot of money) one can achieve anything. She wrote plays, poetry and lyrics; she commissioned original material, financially supported young and emerging musicians, designed stage sets and costumes, hired out halls and personally sold tickets to ensure that those same halls were filled to capacity. She took on the most challenging vocal pieces imaginable and made them her own.

Florence Foster Jenkins was a woman who knew how to make things happen. She had persistence and she was a go-getter; above all she completely believed in herself. *Life* magazine wrote of her 'unquenchable ambition to sing', which, the author attested, 'triumphed over what was probably the most complete and absolute lack of talent ever publicly displayed in Manhattan'.[7] Narcissa was a narcissist in the truest sense of the word.

There were abysmal performers before her – including the atrocious Cherry Sisters, who trod the boards around the turn of the twentieth century with their appalling vaudeville act and were reputedly pelted with everything from rotten vegetables to a broken washing machine for their troubles – but none has left behind the recorded legacy she has: nine tracks of light opera and art songs (vocal compositions written to be performed as part of a recital, unlike those written as part of a musical or stage show), recorded in a short burst of creativity during the Second World War, all performed in her inimitable, tuneless style. Other dreadful singers have followed in her wake – Anna Russell (who actually could sing, but whose decision to make a career out of mauling Mozart was directly inspired by seeing Madame perform), the silent movie star turned pop pugilist Leona Anderson, Mrs. Miller, whose off-key rendition of *Downtown* bruised the singles charts in the mid-1960s, the Hong Kong-born Wing and American Idol reject William Hung, to name a few – but none have captured the public's imagination in quite the same way as Florence. *Billboard* magazine, reviewing her posthumous release *A Florence! Foster!! Jenkins!!! Recital!!!!*, said that 'listening to her pathetic bleating is something like eavesdropping on a padded cell inmate'.[8] Their readers disagreed, sending the album high into the classical charts; her recordings are still available to this day.

'What she provided was never exactly an aesthetic experience, or only to the degree that an early Christian among the lions provided an aesthetic experience,' wrote William Meredith in *The Hudson Review*. 'It was chiefly immolatory, and Madame Jenkins was always eaten in the end.'[9]

We live in a society that laps up the mundane: thanks to TV shows such as The X Factor, Britain's Got Talent and the like our homes are invaded by bad singers on a weekly basis, and today it seems as if anyone can become a star for a week or two, although that very same celebrity is as disposable as a blunt razor. Florence wasn't just a bad singer: we have evidence that proves that she was a stratospherically, catastrophically awful one. And yet it was her limitations that catapulted her to real, lasting stardom and to ceaseless celebrity. Bad singers usually bring out feelings of revulsion, pity or disgust thanks to their dreadfully off-pitch squealing, but Florence never fails to make the listener smile, to elicit feelings of genuine warmth towards her. As St. Clair Bayfield, her lover,

One of Florence's favourite photographs: taken in New York, it appeared in several newspapers and periodicals in the mid 1930s.

manager and unflinching supporter, once put it: 'She only ever thought of making other people happy.'[10]

Irving Hoffman, of the *Hollywood Reporter*, may have observed (correctly) that 'most of her notes were promissory',[11] but there can be no doubt that she was the real deal, and that we shall never see her like again. As Daniel Dixon wrote in his famous article 'The Diva of Din', 'She had a superb faith in her destiny as a diva. She was tireless. She was genuine. And she was indomitable. Neither she nor the vision she clung to could be squelched. In the end Madame Jenkins was more than a joke. She was also an eloquent lesson in fidelity and courage.'[12]

If Florence were plying her trade today this sour soprano would be a major star. Millions would have watched her YouTube videos and her audition for American Idol would be the stuff of legend. It's our misfortune that – unless the long-lost film footage of her in performance is ever rediscovered – we shall never get to appreciate her in her full, unbridled glory, and will never know the genuine joy that she brought to an audience.

1 Welcome to Wilkes-Barre

Settled in 1769 and named after British politicians Isaac Barré and John Wilkes, two of the most notable champions of the American colonies in the Houses of Parliament, the city of Wilkes-Barre reached the height of its prosperity in the nineteenth century, earning its nickname 'The Diamond City' thanks to its position at the centre of Pennsylvania's rich anthracite coal-fields. Located in the middle of the Wyoming Valley, the city expanded quickly: hundreds of thousands of immigrants came in search of work and made the area around Wilkes-Barre their home and, although you wouldn't know it now, as the local economy flourished it rose to become one of the great industrial cities of the United States. It was just the right place for an ambitious and upwardly mobile young man like Charles Dorrance Foster to make his mark.

Descended from British settlers, the lineage of the Foster family can be traced all the way back to Sir Richard Forester, who fought at the Battle of Hastings alongside William the Conqueror (several historians have recorded that Richard was the son of Baldwin V of Flanders and William's brother-in-law, although this is disputed by others). At one time or another a schoolmaster, a lawyer, a banker and a member of the Pennsylvania legislature, Charles Dorrance Foster was born in November 1836 in the township of Dallas, Pennsylvania (the 1900 census records his birth year, incorrectly, as 1838), and his 'boyhood days were occupied in attending the district schools during the winter months and working on the farm in summer'.[1] Despite being the only child and sole heir of Phineas Nash Foster, 'a prosperous farmer of Jackson Township near Huntsville'[2] and 'a prominent Justice of the Peace',[3] and his wife Mary Bailey Johnson Foster (known in the family as Polly, who already had three children – Charles' half-siblings – from a previous marriage), Charles by no means saw his future in farming.

When he was twenty years old he bade the family farm goodbye. Before her marriage his mother had been a teacher and Charles chose to follow in her footsteps, training as a schoolmaster at the Wyoming Seminary in Kingston, Pennsylvania, founded by the Methodist Church in 1844. He studied there for three years before leaving to teach at schools in Jackson Township and in Illinois. Although he was a dedicated educator, Charles Dorrance Foster had ambitions beyond the classroom: he wanted to make something of himself.

Moving to the rapidly expanding city of Wilkes-Barre, Charles joined the office of Lyman Hakes, a local attorney, and was admitted to the bar in April 1861. His

Charles Dorrance Foster, Florence's father.

burgeoning law career was put on hold when, in the summer of 1862, more than a year into the American Civil War, he 'joined a company of home guards, shouldered a musket, marched with the Pennsylvania militia into Maryland and stood ready to defend the integrity of the commonwealth.'[4] He soon saw action. On 17 September Robert E. Lee and George McClellan faced off near Antietam Creek in Sharpsburg, Maryland. With more than 22,000 casualties, the Battle of Antietam is remembered as the bloodiest single-day battle in American history. Charles was one of the lucky ones:

he survived the war and on 4 October 1865, just a few months after the cessation of hostilities, he married a young woman by the name of Mary Jane Hoagland in Newark, New Jersey.

Born in February 1840,[5] Mary was the granddaughter of Judge Andrew Hoagland, a man she would proudly claim to have been one of the earliest slave-holders in the US to free his slaves, decades in advance of the Emancipation Proclamation and the adoption of the Thirteenth Amendment to the United States Constitution. Her family originated in Holland: one of her ancestors, Dirck Jansen Hoagland (incorrectly identified in *Foster Genealogy* as Dirck Hanse Hoagland), built the first brick house on Manhattan Island[6] and, along with two of his wife's brothers, founded the village that would become Bedford, NY. Her father, Amos, was closely tied to the Episcopal church: he built a chapel in Sergentsville, New Jersey, which he gave to the local congregation, and was said to be 'a man of considerable wealth, noted for his generosity to the poor'.[7] A keen amateur artist, in later life Mary won prizes for her landscape paintings (although the *Encyclopedia of American Biography*'s claim that she was a 'famous artist' is rather over-egging this particular pudding), and she came with a considerable dowry.

As a partner in Foster and Lewis Attorneys at Law, Charles shared an office with Thomas H.B. Lewis that, from around 1875, was situated adjacent to the Foster

Mary Jane Hoagland Foster, Florence's mother.

family home on South Franklin Street, Wilkes-Barre. He was 'a reliable and successful lawyer', according to the *Wilkes-Barre Record*,[8] and over the next few decades he would also become the president of the Wilkes-Barre and Kingston Passenger Railway Company (in February 1867; the WB & K was the first street railway, or tram system, in Wilkes-Barre), a director of the Wyoming National Bank (handily located just a stone's throw from the family home on the corner of South Franklin and Market Streets), treasurer of the Wyoming Building and Loan Association, director of the Wilkes-Barre and Dallas Turnpike Company, and treasurer of the Hunlock Creek Turnpike Company. A shrewd investor, he snapped up local real estate to help build the family fortune and was not averse to borrowing money when he saw an opportunity. He had no qualms about profiting from the misfortune of others by purchasing property that had been foreclosed: in October 1872, for example, he purchased the estate of one John L. Yocum at a sheriff's sale, and in this way he built a sizeable portfolio of real estate, employing a manager to collect rents on his behalf.

Upon his father's death in 1878 he inherited the family farm and, although he maintained ownership, its day-to-day running was left to William Bulford, a relative through Charles's mother's first marriage to Captain Albon Bulford. 'Though his business is strictly that of a lawyer with large practice, he takes great pleasure in overseeing and managing his large farm,' according to the *History of Luzerne, Lackawanna and Wyoming Counties,*[9] 'and makes frequent visits with his fine team of horses; not only as a matter of business but also to gratify his filial devotion to his aged mother, who still resides at the modest farm-house where she has spent the greater part of her long life'.[10] H.C. Bradsby's *History of Luzerne County* states that 'having inherited an area of more than a mile of choice farmland in Dallas and Jackson townships, he found that possession sufficient to occupy most of his time and for all of his wants. So he gave only incidental attention to legal practice.'[11]

A staunch Republican, Charles was nominated for the Lower House of the State Legislature in 1882 (he had failed to win his party's backing two years previously) for the First District of Luzerne and Lackawanna, but was defeated by one Herman C. Fry. Two years later Charles Foster was his party's candidate again, and this time he was elected. That same year he came within fifteen votes of being nominated for Congress. Ironically his business partner, Thomas Lewis, had previously been a candidate for the Democratic Party.

Status, possessions and all the trappings of wealth were important to Charles, and he instilled in his wife (and, later, his daughter) the value of belonging to the right societies. He was a member of more than a dozen clubs and associations including the Elks (an organisation similar to the Masons, to which he also belonged, although with less interest in religious cultism and better access to booze), the Wilkes-Barre State National Bar Association, the Wyoming Historical and Geological Society (both he and Mary were life members), the State and National Bankers' Association, the Wyoming Commemorative Monuments' Association and the New England Society. As would be expected of a family whose social status and bank balance were rising, the Fosters kept domestic servants, and at least one resided alongside the family at 27 South Franklin Street: Sarah Phoenix, Evelyn Hertzell, Amy Trim and a labourer named Edward Getty all lived at the family home at one time or another.

'Mr. Foster is a man of fine physique, and in the enjoyment of robust health. He is, as yet, a comparatively

The Foster family lived at 27 South Franklin Street, Wilkes-Barre.

young man, and is the possessor of wealth ample to gratify anything short of sordid avarice,' wrote George Kulp. 'Few men enjoy, at so early an age, such complete physical, financial, and social advantages. It is not matter for wonder, therefore, that he is possessed of a most agreeable temper, and many other qualities that combine to make him a good friend and a delightful companion.'[12] It was into this life of wealth, privilege and comfort that, on 19 July 1868, Narcissa Florence Foster was born.

The Fosters doted on their attractive and vivacious daughter and, like most young women of that period from well-to-do families, she was schooled in music and elocution. The Fosters were overjoyed when Mary became pregnant for a second time, presenting the seven-year-old Florence with a baby sister, Lillian Blanche (known to the family as Lilly). Papa Foster adored both of his daughters, and when he could afford the time he would hitch up his horses and carriage and take them both to Harveys Lake, a popular summer resort some sixteen miles from their home, for the weekend. Florence was dedicated to her piano lessons and showed a real aptitude for music, and within twelve months of Lilly's arrival she gave her first concerts, billed as 'Little Miss Foster'. Considered a musical prodigy, before she was a teenager Florence is said to have played at the White House. She appeared as a member of a centennial Chorus of some five hundred local people in front of

President Rutherford B. Hayes when he visited Wilkes-Barre in 1878 to commemorate the hundredth anniversary of the Battle of Wyoming. The President drew a crowd of some 50,000 to hear him speak, and it's more than likely that Little Miss Foster would have been introduced to the President after the performance – as a prominent local figure Papa Foster was connected to the organising committee and would later serve the on the board of the Wyoming Commemorative Association – and that he invited the talented young pianist to come and play for him at his official residence, then known as the Executive Mansion. Florence's paternal grandmother also took part in the centenary celebrations.

On at least two occasions Florence performed as a soloist at säengerfests, music festivals that took place annually at different cities around the country and involved hundreds of amateur singers and choirs. The säengerfests were monumental occasions: the host city would be decked out in bunting, store windows would be filled with colourful displays, musical events would take place throughout the area and the climax of the three-day festival – an all-day outdoor concert – attracted thousands of visitors from outside the region. In 1881 the grand finale was held in the City Hall Gardens, Wilkes-Barre, and Florence, who opened the second half of the day's musical programme with a piano solo entitled *Polonaise*, was singled out for her 'mastery of the instrument, lightness of touch and rapid action. It was a bright and lively selection and Miss Foster's playing was vigorously applauded."[13] The approval of the audience was ambrosia to Florence: she thirsted for and lapped up the acclaim and, when the opportunity presented itself, she willingly left the family home to pursue her studies.

2 Mrs. Doctor Jenkins

A precocious and restless child with a thirst for knowledge, Florence was frustrated by the meagre excuse for an education being offered to her at home. Young ladies from well-to-do families were discouraged from attempting to achieve any kind of scholastic qualifications as in those days it was almost unheard of for a woman to be educated. Opportunities for women in educational institutions were scarce, yet such Victorian attitudes were slowly changing, and around the middle of the century more and more private schools for girls, known as seminaries, were springing up around the country. Florence was adamant that she was not going to be denied an education, her grandmother and father had both been teachers after all, and when she was in her teens her parents agreed to send her to boarding school in Philadelphia.

Philadelphia, the third largest city in the United States at the time, was much more cosmopolitan than the town she had grown up in, and much more open to new ideas. Diverse ethnic groups were scattered throughout the city, libraries, museums and theatres abounded, and young Florence greedily lapped up the culture on offer.

Popular with her fellow students, she quickly settled in to life at the West Walnut Street Seminary for Young Ladies, presided over by Mrs. Henrietta Kutz and noted for 'giving a superior education' in many subjects, including music and the arts. She graduated in 1883, winning a gold medal for elocution. The keen scholar also excelled in her lessons at the Philadelphia Musical Academy, passing her piano classes with the highest honours. Buoyed by her success, Florence looked forward to returning to Wilkes-Barre for the summer, yet any celebrations that may have been planned by the

Florence excelled in her piano lessons at the Philadelphia Musical Academy.

family for her remarkable scholastic achievements were cut cruelly short.

Throughout the decade outbreaks of diphtheria were rife in the region and, just weeks after Florence graduated from Mrs. Kutz's Seminary, her adored sister Lilly died, aged eight, of the disease. 'The little one, so suddenly called away in the very midst of the bright days of childhood, had won her way deep into the hearts of all who knew her', declared the florid notice that appeared under the heading 'The Hand of Death' in the *Wilkes-Barre Record*. 'She was of a joyous and kindly disposition, and had given ample evidence of the possession of still nobler qualities which would have made her life one of great promise.'[1] She was buried on 1 July in the cemetery at Huntsville. Her remains – and those of her paternal grandparents – were later re-interred at the family mausoleum in Wilkes-Barre's Hollenback cemetery, which Charles Foster had built in 1900.

Understandably the death of Lilly affected the family deeply and, perhaps unsurprisingly, when Florence expressed a desire to go abroad to continue her musical studies and, it is presumed, further them by also taking singing lessons, her father refused to let her go. Her formative years playing piano for appreciative audiences had instilled in her the unwavering conviction that she was destined to be a star, but as far as Charles Foster was concerned, Florence's lot was to be married and raise children, to teach in school or to remain at home and look after her parents in their dotage. According to Cosme McMoon, the man who would become her best-known accompanist, both Charles and Mary were vehemently opposed to Florence ever singing in public because 'her parents objected to the excruciating quality of her voice'. As the scion of a well-to-do family, and with a father as starchily Victorian and middle-class as Charles Foster was, it would have been improper for Florence to perform before a paying public. Music was all right as a distraction; it was not an occupation, and he refused to pay for such an extravagance.

With no income of her own, Florence had no option but to acquiesce. Unless she could find someone else to support her financially, of course.

Stories abound about the young Miss Foster eloping to Philadelphia and marrying in 1886, yet within twelve months of Lilly's death Florence was already using her married name. On 5 October 1884 the entire Foster family were nearly killed when Charles lost control of the horse-drawn carriage in which they, along with a Doctor Johnson, were riding. All four occupants were thrown from the carriage when it turned over, with Mary Foster fracturing her left arm. Luckily the others, Florence included, sustained only minor injuries. Reports of the accident made several local newspapers, where she is referred to as Mrs. Dr. Jenkins. Further press reports from 1885 have her already living in Philadelphia with her husband. There is no mention anywhere of an elopement before 1954, when Cosme McMoon, interviewed by RCA's Chick Crumpacker, stated that 'in her early teens she ran away from home and went to Philadelphia to try and make her way'. Like so much of what we think we know about her, it appears that this part of Florence's legend was an invention – either by McMoon or, far more likely, by Florence herself. Few of the so-called facts of her early life stand up to close scrutiny; she was adept at embroidering her personal history to make it more colourful, and many of the creative embellishments she employed for her biography have gone down in history as unimpeachable truth.

Doctor Francis 'Frank' Thornton Jenkins was the son of Rear Admiral Thornton Alexander Jenkins, who had been an officer in the United States Navy during both the Mexican-American War and the American Civil War, and who is said to have worked covertly for President Abraham Lincoln. Born in Baltimore in 1852, he followed his father and maternal grandfather, Francis Anthony Thornton, into the navy where he enjoyed a distinguished career before leaving to take up private practice. One of Frank's sisters was the noted suffragette Alice Carlton Jenkins, delegate for the District of Columbia at three national American Woman Suffrage Conventions. Frank also held office within the Lighthouse Engineers of Philadelphia, according to a report in the *Wilkes-Barre Record*, 'largely owing not only to his ability but to the fact that his habits have always been strictly temperate, and in consequence [he] could endure more fatigue than those who held positions above him',[2] suggesting perhaps that his colleagues were more than fond of a drink or two.

Although he was a generation older than her, Frank and Florence had become close during her time at school in Philadelphia. Frank had studied at the University of Pennsylvania, just yards away from Mrs. Kutz's seminary, and practised in hospitals in both Philadelphia and Washington D.C., where Alice and another sister, Sarah, shared a home. Sixteen years Florence's senior, he had already been engaged at least once before (in August 1882 to Miss Kate Henry) yet, in spite of her father's misgivings, she married him even though she herself was just sixteen – and in those days the average age at which a woman married was twenty-two. Charles Foster may have disapproved of his daughter's choice of beau, especially as Dr. Jenkins was an active Democrat, but at least he had a respectable career and could be expected to take care of her.

The newlyweds set up home at 1920 Franklin Street, Philadelphia. She may have been the young wife of a successful doctor now, but Florence fully intended to continue her musical studies. She enrolled at Ida Heyl's School of Vocal Art on Chestnut Street, and would graduate head of the class from the Philadelphia Conservatory of Music in 1888. Once again she stood out, being rated second out of the eight hundred students there: 'Mrs.

Jenkins is a brilliant musician and is so considered in classical circles. She is very popular in social circles; her many friends here will be glad to learn of her success.'[3]

The accepted story has it that Charles disinherited Florence when she took up with Frank, but reports of an enforced estrangement from her parents all seem to stem from articles written after her death. As Florence's cousin Nancy Elston Schimmel says: 'I feel certain that she was not estranged from her parents. Having lost one daughter, they were not likely to disown the remaining one.' The new Dr. and Mrs. Jenkins were hardly strangers, becoming regular visitors to the Foster family home. Frank was there in July 1884 (in the first press reference to him as 'son in law of C.D. Foster'[4]): Mary, Charles Foster's mother, had taken ill and her grandson-in-law was helping care for her. Sadly she died on 23 July at eighty-eight years of age. He visited South Franklin Street again in both August and September. The whole family spent Christmas and New Year 1885 together in Wilkes-Barre, and Charles and Mary would also visit with Frank and Florence, spending a week at their home in Philadelphia in May 1886.

Frank and Florence may have put on a façade of respectability, but it appears that theirs was a miserable marriage. Although they gave the impression of being inseparable during the first two years of matrimony, by the summer of 1886 Florence was travelling alone: she joined her parents in Saratoga for their summer vacation that year, registering at the United States Hotel – one of the resort's most luxurious and expensive establishments – as Mrs. Dr. Jenkins. Florence seems to have left Frank on several occasions, each time returning home to her parents. After one of their earliest separations, in September 1886, Charles Foster accompanied his headstrong daughter back to Philadelphia to effect a reconciliation or, perhaps, to threaten Frank with legal action if he did not treat his wife correctly. It is clear that he was unfaithful to her: Florence is rumoured to have caught syphilis from Frank and the treatment, which in those days involved ingesting a mixture of mercury and arsenic, caused her to go bald and may well have affected her state of mind. Many years later the sculptor Florence Malcolm Darnault recalled inadvertently seeing Madame Jenkins' 'completely bald, shiny, polished' pate. Florence would seek more and more time away from her husband: in 1887 she spent most of the summer out of Philadelphia, vacationing in Montreal and at Harveys Lake, again with her parents.

By the middle of 1889 things had become so difficult between the pair that Frank left Philadelphia, first setting up a practice in Atlanta, Georgia before shuffling off to Buffalo in New York State and opening up an office there. He left Buffalo in 1898 and moved to Niagara Falls, advertising in the local paper as a 'specialist in [the] treatment of diseases of [the] throat, nose, ear and lungs'. The *Buffalo Medical Journal* of September

1898 confirmed this: 'Dr. Frank Thornton Jenkins, of Buffalo, has opened offices at Niagara Falls, N.Y., where he has taken up his residence for the future. He limits his practice to the treatment of diseases of the nose, throat and ear, for which purpose he has fitted up a handsome suite of offices in the Gluck building, Niagara Falls.' He joined the Niagara Falls Academy of Medicine, writing papers on his specialty and presenting them at the society's regular meetings.

Florence began divorce proceedings against Frank in August 1902 (a note in St. Clair Bayfield's diary dates the divorce to 24 March 1902, but this is incorrect). Either she was unaware that Frank was now practising in Niagara Falls, or she and her solicitor, Philippus Miller, decided not to try too hard to track him down: Miller took out a notice that ran for several weeks in the *Buffalo Evening News* to notify the errant Doctor Jenkins that 'Narcissa F. Jenkins, your wife, has instituted proceedings against you, asking for a divorce from the bonds of matrimony on the ground of wilful and malicious desertion'. Frank was invited, via the notice, to attend Miller's office, on South 12th Street, Philadelphia, 'on Wednesday, September 8, 1902, at 11 o'clock on which day you may show cause, if any you have, why such divorce should not be granted against you'. Frank does not appear to have contested the case, if in fact he was aware of the suit against him. Florence was soon free of her wayward husband, and by the beginning of 1905 he had relocated once again, this time to the family home in Washington.

The divorce would have left Florence in Philadelphia alone and without an income. Things in Wilkes-Barre were bad too: a lengthy and drawn-out strike by coal miners over long hours, poor wages and shocking living conditions, later referred to as 'the most important single incident in the labor movement in the United States',[5] had brought the local economy to its knees and tens of thousands left the region.

To make ends meet the newly single Mrs. Jenkins – now using the surname Foster Jenkins – moved to the Newport Apartments building on 16th and Spruce Street and attempted to earn a living as a music teacher and piano player. Feted in the local press as 'one of Philadelphia's most noted performers on the piano',[6] any dreams Florence may have had of success as a concert pianist were dashed when she sustained an injury to her arm. There's no confirmation anywhere as to what this mysterious injury was or what had caused it, unless the injuries she sustained in the coach accident in 1884 were more severe than originally reported, but something certainly prevented her from earning much, if any, money, and she does not appear to have played before a paying audience during this time. She wasn't exactly destitute, however: over the New Year holiday in 1903 Florence could somehow afford to vacation at Laurel-in-the-Pines on the shores of Lake Carasaljo in Lakewood, New Jersey, one of the area's most luxurious hotels and a magnet for the rich and famous, and she managed to spend the summer that year and the following year too in Rhode Island. She may not have had much money – and what little she had must have come from her parents – but she could certainly look the part: 'One of the prettiest girls seen here this season is Miss Florence Foster Jenkins of Philadelphia,' gushed the *New York Press* in January 1903. 'Miss Jenkins was said to be the most beautifully gowned woman at the New Year's Ball in the Laurel House. She wore rare old rose point lace over a pearl colored mousseline de sole. This lace is an heirloom and it was the envy of all the women.'[7] She and Frank may no longer have been

Florence at the piano, surrounded by flowers.

a couple, but Florence kept up appearances and maintained her social commitments, spending a few days in Washington with the Pennsylvania delegation of the patriotic women's organisation, the Daughters of the American Revolution.

When her father discovered that she had parted from Frank and was living in what, to him, must have appeared near-poverty he took it upon himself to visit his delinquent daughter and demand that she return to Wilkes-Barre. Florence does not appear to have revealed to her parents that the couple had divorced, presumably either because her fiercely religious mother frowned upon such a thing, or because the humiliation of a divorce would have hurt the family's social standing. It's possible that this is the reason why, in several press reports following her father's death, she is still referred to as the wife of Dr. Frank Thornton Jenkins of Philadelphia, and in her own short obituary in the *The Sun* (New York) she is referred to as 'the widow of Dr. Frank Thornton Jenkins of Washington. D.C.'[8] which would suggest that they had not divorced before Frank passed away, even though they clearly had. It would also have been in Florence's character to play down the divorce, as she would have enjoyed the snob appeal of being related to Rear Admiral Jenkins, a decorated war hero.

The thought of having a divorcee in the family may have been scandalous, but it could not have been as terrible as having a murderer for a relative: Frank's nephews, the writer Thornton Jenkins Haines and the naval officer Captain Peter C. Haines, would stand trial for the murder of publisher William Annis at the Bayside Yacht Club, Long Island in August 1908. The crime was one of the most notorious cases of its day, and made front-page news across the country. Thornton (no stranger to scandal, he had also been acquitted of shooting a man named Edward A. Hannigan some seventeen years earlier) was acquitted in January 1909, but Peter was convicted of manslaughter and sent to Sing Sing prison. Although he was later pardoned, Florence must have been relieved that she had the foresight to part legally from the Jenkins' clan and therefore distance herself and her parents from potentially ruinous tittle-tattle.

The prodigal daughter was encouraged to return to the family fold, on the strict understanding that she abandoned any interest in becoming a professional musician. After spending Christmas at the family home a browbeaten Florence reluctantly agreed. But it would not be long before her aspirations surfaced again.

Florence was not happy staying put in Wilkes-Barre. Despite her father's misgivings – and the mysterious unexplained arm injury – she was keen to continue her musical studies. In what may have been an attempt to discover a new métier, she began to visit New York on a regular basis. As Charles Foster's tight grip on her movements relaxed (along with his grasp on his wallet), these occasional visits became more frequent and lasted longer and longer. By 1906 she had joined her first New York women's club – the Dickens Fellowship – and even had an address in the city: contemporary directories list her as residing at 18 West 25th Street, the site of the Arlington Hotel near the iconic Flatiron Building, while maintaining her Newport Apartments home in Philadelphia (she was listed as still living at that address in the 1908 Daughters of the American Revolution directory). Before too long she had made enough contacts in New York to start performing, initially as a pianist, for a musical society called the Euterpe Club (she accompanied a recitation by club member Mrs. Vaughan on New Year's Eve 1906), an association that would provide Florence with a springboard from which she would be able to launch her career. Within twelve months of her parents rescuing her from penury she was practically a full-time resident of the great metropolis, and within another year she was programming concerts and recitals as 'chairman of music' for the Euterpe Club.

To improve her ability to project on stage Florence enrolled in the Henry Gaines Hawn School of Speech Arts, which held classes in Carnegie Hall and in Brooklyn, and specialised in diction for singers; Florence and Henry Hawn would later act together in front of the New Yorkers Society, another of the many clubs of which Florence was a member. She also kept up her piano studies at the A.K. Virgil School of Music on Madison Avenue. Things weren't easy – in 1907 Florence landed in court, charged with unpaid debts – but, thanks almost entirely to her father's altruism, she managed to get by in the big city. In September 1909, however, she was summoned home from her summer vacation in Newport, Rhode Island, for what would be the last time.

Charles Dorrance Foster passed away in the early hours of the morning of 9 September. He had been ill for some time: 'his illness dates back a year or more,' according to his obituary in the *Wilkes-Barre Record*, 'when he was afflicted with kidney trouble. An operation afforded him only temporary relief and his condition had been quite serious. In an effort to improve his condition he was taken to Cuba and Florida, and later to the mountains at Wernersville, PA.'[9] It is said that his estate amounted to more than $1.5 million (equivalent to around $40 million in 2015). His will, however, was nowhere to be found.

3 The Curious Case of the Missing Will

'Prominent Lawyer and Citizen Summoned to His Reward' ran the headline in the *Wilkes-Barre Record*, broadcasting the passing of the honourable Charles Dorrance Foster. His funeral was announced for Friday 1 October 1909 at St Stephen's Church, no more than a stone's throw from the family home, before his remains were to be interred in the Foster mausoleum at the Hollenback cemetery. But what the effusive obituary did not report was that his will, penned some six years before his death, had mysteriously vanished.

According to Mary Foster, Charles kept a copy of his Last Will and Testament – written in 1903 but based on a document drawn up several years earlier by Judge Rhone – in the safe in his office. However when she and the family's attorney John McGahren, who shared the office with Foster in the family home, went to look for it the will could not be found. What followed would be months of protracted discussions, arguments, accusations and a major court case to prove that Charles Foster's widow and daughter had a right to inherit his substantial estate.

The first hearing took place on 7 October in front of deputy registrar Peter McCormick. McGahren, a former District Attorney who had trained for the bar under Foster and Lewis and had been a partner in Charles Foster's business for five years, was one of the principal witnesses in the court case. He testified that he 'drew up the document, witnessed the signing and was familiar with the disposition of the estate',[1] and told reporters that only a few days before the will disappeared he 'had it in his possession and read over the various items'.[2] Moreover he would testify that the will had been stolen from a locked safe to which he had the only set of keys. McGahren reported to the court that, on returning to his office from Charles Foster's funeral, he 'found a number of distant relatives of Mr. Foster' waiting for him. On opening the safe door to retrieve the will and read it he 'found the inner doors locked and the key which had always remained in the lock was missing'.[3] A locksmith was called and the inner doors were drilled, but when they finally got the safe open the papers that McGahren had expected to find there were gone. Several of Charles Foster's relatives would later testify on oath that Mary Foster was not in the least bit surprised that there was no will in the safe.

McGahren claimed to have a clear recollection of the contents of the will, and it was hoped that his oral testimony would suffice as evidence of Charles Foster's intentions. Mary Foster agreed with McGahren's recollections of the contents of the will, and within a couple of days a codicil that Charles Foster had apparently composed in January 1909 was located by one of McGahren's associates which seemed to back up this verbal version of the will. All would have been fine had Florence not put a huge spanner in the works when, in December, she filed a paper to the court claiming that when he signed the newly discovered amendment to the will her father 'was not of a sound, disposing mind sufficient to execute such a codicil, and that undue influence was exercised on him by William Bulford [who stood to inherit the Foster family farm] and John McGahren'.[4] Siding with her imperious daughter, Mary Foster quickly turned on her own attorney and told the court that she frequently saw Bulford and McGahren together. Florence testified that she was at the family home when her father died, had no knowledge of any will and that on the date that the disputed codicil was signed she 'was with my father that day all morning. I went to the dentist at noon and was with him again during the afternoon. That day he was in a sleepy condition and did not rouse during the afternoon. John McGahren came into the room that day, talked in a loud and boisterous manner, but it did not rouse my father. He spoke so loud; as if he was addressing a jury.'[5]

Florence was adamant that her father was too ill to have composed the disputed codicil to his will, or altered any extant papers. She made it clear to the court that

his mind was confused and that he may have been hal-
lucinating: 'On the 14th of September he wanted a ham-
mock with his name on it; said he wanted to fly in it,'
she told the judge.[6] She stated that, in her opinion, her
father was not in a sound mind towards the end of his
life, and that he had been incapable of signing his name,
even though cheques bearing his signature – and apparently completed by Mary Foster – had been cashed at the
bank. Charles Foster's personal physician, Dr. Brooke,
stated that he attended his patient two or three times
daily in the last two weeks of his life and that, in his
judgment, he was lucid and would not have been easily
coerced. Testimony was made that McGahren, incensed
at this turn of events, had threatened Florence, saying
that 'before he was through with her he would make her
crawl on her knees before him'.[7]

As the case trundled on the court learned that the
Fosters' home life was often tempestuous, that Charles
Foster almost certainly had enjoyed the company of a
mistress or two during their marriage, and that on the
day of his funeral Florence was discovered 'upstairs cry-
ing her eyes out because she thought Mr. Foster cut her
out of his will and did not leave her a cent'.[8] Florence
admitted to the court that her father and mother had
some 'spats', and that she had tried to stop her mother
from reading the bible to her father and took the book
away from her. The court heard how, in his last days,
Charles Foster 'was in a helpless condition, very weak

and nervous, and unable to leave his bed'.[9] It was suggested by John Garman, the attorney who took over the representation of Florence and Mary, that Charles had been conducting an affair with a woman by the name of Mae V. Smith, the daughter of one of his business associates, and that Florence had seen the pair kissing. Mae, who stood to inherit $1,000 from the will (quite a substantial amount in those days), had been a frequent visitor to the Foster house during the latter days of Charles's life, had accompanied the Foster family on a trip to the then popular and exclusive resort of Atlantic City in May 1908, and had also been with Charles and Mary on their trip to Cuba during his convalescence. Florence, Garman revealed to the scandalised court, had refused to go to Cuba with her parents because Mae Smith was there, and had also declined to join them for dinner in Atlantic City because Smith was seated at the same table.

The case had already been dragging through the court for more than a year – with twenty-five lawyers (including three former District Attorneys, two judges and an ex-member of the House of Representatives) reportedly involved at one point – when, in October 1910, the earliest copy of the will, the version that Charles Foster had had drawn up by Judge Rhone, was anonymously posted to the office of the Wilkes-Barre People's Bank. Days later a mutilated copy of the 1903 will, in Charles Foster's own handwriting, was delivered to John McGahren. Both versions of the will had been posted, on the same day, from New York. The *Wilkes-Barre Record* made much of the fact that the envelopes containing the wills were addressed with printed letters so that the sender could not be traced through his (or her) handwriting: the parts which had been crudely cut from the 1903 will were later sent to John Garman, who by that point was acting as court-appointed administrator of the Foster estate. Proceedings were complicated further by mention of a bequest to Foster's half-sister Olive Manville, who had died several years before the 1903 will was written. McGahren insisted that this was an oversight that happened when he, on Charles Foster's instruction, had copied sections from the Judge Rhone-produced will verbatim. A contemporary newspaper reported that 'several arrests will follow the return of the wills'.[10]

When Charles's estate was finally settled it was decided that the bequests he had made, which incorporated gifts of $500 each to the Home for Homeless Women in Wilkes-Barre and to the Luzerne County Humane Association for the Prevention of Cruelty to Aged Persons, Children and Animals plus amounts of between $250 and $1,000 to the people, including Mae Smith, who had been 'been very kind to me in sickness', should stand. Foster's arrangements to ensure that his half-sister was taken care of were void; his other half-siblings were not mentioned in any version of the will as both had died before the first draft was completed:

Florence photographed in her hotel suite, shortly after she moved to New York.

Lord Butler Bulford, his eldest half-brother, had died in 1860; his other half-sibling John Jacob Bulford in November 1897. Other amendments to the will were judged invalid.

Florence need not have worried about being disinherited: Charles left her his diamond stud and his piano.
He also left amounts varying from $50 to $100 to many
friends, relatives and godchildren. The will included
a bequest of $1,000 for a window – to be designed by
Florence and Mary – to be installed in St Stephen's
Episcopal Church in memory of Lilly Foster. Everything
that was left was to be 'paid quarterly to my wife Mary J.
Foster and my daughter Florence in equal shares during
their lives, and to the survivor of them after the death
of either'. William Bulford, who had testified against
Florence and Mary in court, was to continue to run
the family farm and pay an annuity of $600 to be split
equally between the two Foster women.

Both his wife and his daughter were now free of
Charles's control, and both were very, very wealthy.

4 Florence and St. Clair

Once a suitable period of mourning had passed Florence moved permanently to the Big Apple, this time taking her mother with her. Mary had strong roots in New York, her ancestors having first arrived there as settlers from the Netherlands in the 1650s; with no family left in Wilkes-Barre, relocating to the big city proved the attractive and obvious thing to do. The Foster family home on South Franklin Street was sold, but the Foster women didn't completely abandon their home town. Mary Foster would continue to support projects that her family had been involved with for the rest of her life: after her husband died she made a number of gifts of books, furniture and other household items to the Wyoming Historical and Geological Society (now known as the Luzerne County Historical Society), donating $1,000 in both 1916 and 1917 (noted in the annual reports of the society as the Charles Dorrance Foster Fund) and, in 1924, a further $5,000 to establish a Memorial Endowment membership in memory of her second daughter, Lillian. That same year the Society reconstructed a colonial log cabin in their Reading Room, and Mary donated many of the props on display there; she even contributed 'artificial flowers for a bonnet, worn by (an) ancestress of Mrs. Charles D. Foster several hundred years ago'.[1] 'During her lifetime she made many donations of money and items to the Wyoming Historical and Geological Society,' Nancy Schimmel confirms. Although nowhere near as munificent towards her hometown as her mother, in 1934 Florence paid for the renovation of a stable and garage on River Street, the same stable where her father had once kept his carriage and horses, just around the corner from the old homestead and close to the Foster family crypt.

In the early years of the twentieth century, New York was very much the place to be. Atlanta, Boston, Chicago and San Francisco may have conquered their respective corners of the United States, but by 1920 more than a quarter of the three hundred largest corporations in America had their headquarters in New York, and the city dominated the entire union in terms of trade, communications, finance and especially culture. Musicians, artists, playwrights and actors from all four corners of the globe passed through the city that the legendary news reporter Walter Cronkite referred to as 'America's front door', and when Florence and Mary decided to sell up in Wilkes-Barre and begin their lives anew in New York it was the only place that two ladies of their social standing, with their interests and with Florence's unfulfilled ambitions, could make any impact.

Both women shared a taste for hotel life, so the two rather wealthy ladies took rooms in different establishments, with Florence making a home for herself initially at the St. Louis Hotel (now the Hotel Grand Union, at 34 East 32nd Street) before settling in suite number 86 at the Hotel Seymour on West 45th Street. The Hotel Seymour had opened for business in October 1905 and as a result of its proximity to the city's theatre district had quickly become a favoured haunt of New York's actors and musicians. The Foster women spent their days socialising and their evenings dining out or at the theatre – one of Florence's earliest extravagances was to reserve a pair of seats for her use each Saturday night at the Metropolitan Opera – and the pair soon became an accepted and integral part of New York society.

Mary and Florence joined (and indeed financed) several clubs, organised salons and soirees, were seen in all the best places and appeared regularly in the society columns of New York newspapers. By the time of her death, Mary had been a member of over forty different clubs and societies. Florence was an officer of more than a dozen organisations, including the National Opera Club (she was the club's official historian), the National Patriotic Society and, most importantly, the Euterpe Club, and a member of a great many more. Presided over by the formidable Mrs. Alcinous Berton Jamison, whose doctor husband was a colorectal specialist, clairvoyant, author and the inventor of the Internal Fountain Bath enema, the Euterpe Club met on Fridays at Carnegie Hall, held monthly receptions in its members' homes and organised four concerts a year. It provided Florence with an entree to New York's musical world.

As well as satisfying her desire to become a diva, Florence had another major reason for wanting to live in New York. On a snowy Thursday morning of 14 January 1909, during one of her earlier extended periods of residence in the city, she had met a young actor by the name of St. Clair Bayfield, a dashingly handsome,

Florence photographed for the *Musical Courier,* 1920.

well-spoken and talented Englishman seven years her junior. The pair first encountered each other at the Waldorf-Astoria hotel, on Fifth Avenue, during a Euterpe Club meeting. They would run into each other again that evening at a party on Riverside Drive, and the pair quickly became inseparable. She would spend the rest of her life with him, and each year on 14 January he would send her flowers to mark the anniversary of the day they first met.

Described in later life as 'a tall, lank man with a bony face, prominent nose, extraordinarily large ears and a headful of long, raggedy, wavy, grayish blonde hair'[2] (he notes in his diary that he stood five foot eleven and three quarter inches and weighed 146 lb), he was born John St. Clair Roberts in Cheltenham, England in 1875, the illegitimate grandson of Edward Law, Earl of Ellenborough, who had been Governor General of India from 1842 to 1844. He had attempted to earn a living as an actor and acting coach in his home town (St. Clair lived at 10 Pittville Lawn, Cheltenham, a fine Georgian property) and in London, where he joined the repertory company of the noted English actor Sir Herbert Beerbohm Tree, before deciding to emigrate to New Zealand in 1901. The New Zealand Theatre Archives hold his diary, which St. Clair titled *A Theatrical Tour through New Zealand and Australia,* covering 15 November 1901 to 12 July 1902. He joined William Hawtrey's English Comedy Company and appeared in a stage version of the hit play *A Message From Mars* at the Criterion Theatre in Sydney in 1903, but acting jobs were few and far between, and to sustain himself he took on other work away from the stage, including a stint as a sheep rancher and as a member of a volunteer regiment called the Waikiki Rifles. He made his first trip to the United States the same year, touring with the Ben Greet

Florence met St. Clair Bayfield in January 1909: they would stay together for the rest of her life (image courtesy of the Billy Rose Theatre Division, New York Public Library).

Players, a troupe managed by the English actor, director, and impresario Sir Philip Barling Greet, in a revival of the fifteenth-century morality play *Everyman* and in Shakespeare's *Twelfth Night*.

America must have seemed a much more attractive, and potentially lucrative, proposition than the antipodes: between March and May 1904, as a member of the Ben Greet Players, he appeared as Gobbo in *The Merchant of Venice*, as the Sea Captain in *Twelfth Night*, as a shepherd in *As You Like It* and as Robin Starveling in *A Midsummer Night's Dream*, as well as the Inn Keeper in Oliver Goldsmith's *She Stoops to Conquer* in New York and Washington. He returned to England briefly, appearing at London's Royal Court Theatre as the March Hare in *Alice*, based on the books by Lewis Carroll, and as an 'old man' in *Beatrice* by Rosina Philippi in 1905, but the following year he was back touring the States once again with Ben Greet and his merry band. His friend William Hawtrey had also relocated to America, and the two of them appeared together in *The Two Mr. Wetherbys* at the Madison Square Theatre (the *New York Daily Tribune* reported that 'St. Clair Bayfield deserves mention for his excellent interpretation of a solemn prig'[3]), and opposite Fritzi Scheff in the comic opera *The Prima Donna* in Chicago. Miss Scheff would remain a lifelong friend and would offer him much support after Florence passed away. Settling in New York, St. Clair, who was described as 'a master of dialects'[4] and who would teach diction when he was 'resting', joined the local chapter of the Actors' Church Alliance (a society set up by Episcopal clergyman and former actor Walter Bentley) and took pretty much any and every role that came his way. At the time he met Florence he was living at a boarding house on West 23rd Street and was, as usual, struggling financially. They were immediately attracted to each other and quickly began to date, attending a function together at the Pleiades Club in Greenwich Village, New York on 24 January. Before they could begin a relationship, however, St. Clair had to make a short trip back to England to terminate his engagement to another woman.

Shockingly for the day, the couple would never officially marry, although according to St. Clair they took part in a ceremonial marriage in front of a handful of close friends at the Hotel Vanderbilt on 16 August that year. 'We made a marriage compact just between ourselves,' he told interviewer Betty Moorsteen of New York's short-lived but hugely influential *PM Daily* newspaper (St. Clair was interviewed on 25 April; the article was published on 30 May 1945). 'We exchanged rings. I gave her my grandmother's wedding band. This is the ring she gave me,' he told her, showing off the gold ring set with a blue lapis lazuli that he wore on the third finger of his left hand. 'She called it a ring of entwining love. Because of her club work she wanted to keep our marriage a secret. My wife was very secretive about everything, anyway. Her singing instructor was a great opera star, but there is only one person in the world who knows the name. Who made all her costumes? No one knows except me.'

Over the years several possible contenders have been put forward as Florence's vocal coach, including Carlo Edwards, the assistant conductor of the Metropolitan Opera who would go on to become a production manager at NBC, and the mezzo soprano Henriette Wakefield, who had sung with Caruso. Madame Wakefield and her husband Greek Evans ran the famous Theatre in the Woods in Norwalk, Connecticut; Florence attended a performance of *The Vagabond King* there in August 1932.

'One time she asked me to play a violin obbligato at her voice lesson,' wrote Mozelle Bennett Sawyer, the noted violinist who was once a member of the Verdi Club Trio. 'While she sang her teacher, a famous opera coach, stood behind her winking at me. She bounced from one opera coach to another, because no one could risk his reputation too long, accepting her money and being amused. She was intelligent about learning arias – but that voice! Words can't describe how terrible it was.'[5] Few of her instructors have ever been confirmed: Albano Seismit-Doda was named as coaching Florence in the *Musical Courier* in November and December 1922, and Miss Grace M. Liddane was outed as one of her coaches by the *Amsterdam Evening Recorder* in

September 1928. Seismit-Doda is also reported to have composed a song for her at her behest, based on their music lessons (she performed a song by Seismit-Doda, entitled *Dream*, at the Pleiades Club at the Brevoort Hotel in November 1922). Florence herself claimed to have studied with the great international pantomime star Madame Pilar-Morin, with New York-based vocal teacher Sergei Klibansky and with the Dutch-born conductor and composer Richard Hageman.

Florence and St. Clair were devoted to each other, and he would act as her manager and general factotum until the day she died, offering her unfailing support, helping her with the staging of her recitals, escorting her to parties, to opening night performances and to the opera. He attempted to keep his own career going, writing the three-act comedy-drama *The Mending of Brinks* (1913) in which he hoped to appear, but looking after Florence quickly became a full-time occupation. He began to write and direct one-act plays that she would present at her various clubs; legitimate acting roles still came, but nowhere near enough to allow him to support himself financially. Most of the productions he appeared in ran from just one night to a maximum of three weeks. It wasn't until 1920 that he managed to land a role in a genuine hit, appearing in *Deburau* with Lionel Atwill. This ran for 189 performances and was quickly followed by his role as James Handley in the Broadway production of *Bulldog Drummond*, which ran for 162 performances. 'Florence could not have functioned without him,' Bill Brady, a friend of Bayfield's, told biographer Gregor Benko during his research for the documentary, *A World of Her Own*. 'It was he who had the taste and talent, and it was the activities that he directed for her that made Florence a person to reckon with in society, not her recitals. She was someone to be reckoned with despite her singing, not because of it.'

It is likely that they chose not to marry as a clause in Charles Foster's will forbade any husband from having control of Florence's inheritance – 'the bequests to my said daughter shall be free from the control of her present or any future husband'[6] – and it is clear that he was unaware of his daughter's divorce from Doctor Jenkins when he wrote his will in November 1903. 'We were never married in the conventional way,' Bayfield confided to Betty Moorsteen. 'My enemy in the whole thing was the fact that she had had a very unhappy first marriage to Frank Thornton Jenkins. She said that if she ever married again it would be a common-law marriage – she was very superstitious about it. She was very superstitious about everything. For instance, I was never allowed to put a hat on the bed. She would never give or accept a present with a point; thought it would break friendship. She wouldn't let me give her a beautiful paperknife once for that reason. And when I went to the dressmaker – I supervised all her fittings for her costumes – she wouldn't let anyone speak while the dressmaker was pinning the garments.'[7]

In October 1917 Florence took on the lease of an apartment at 66 West 37th Street (the original building has long since gone, replaced by an ugly office block), funding a home for St. Clair in rather drab rented rooms above the showroom of the Mascot Talking Machine Company. This would have been the perfect time for Florence and St. Clair to cement their relationship with an official marriage, but for some reason known only to them, despite the fact that Mary Foster adored St. Clair (she always called him Mr. Roberts, his surname at birth, and often asked him when he was going to make an honest women of her daughter; St. Clair often spoke of Mary, Florence and himself as 'our little trio'), Florence was dead against it. Once again, St. Clair simply put this decision down to superstition.

In keeping with the unconventional nature of their relationship, although the couple maintained these rooms (St. Clair always referred to the apartment as their 'studio') they would seldom receive guests there nor would they admit that these were, in fact, their married quarters. Each Christmas one or two of their closest friends were invited for a small drinks party and to help trim their tree which, in the early years, was lit with real candles, but that was as far as it went. Florence continued to pay the rent on her suite and St. Clair moved some of his belongings in there; the Hotel Seymour remained her official residence until the day she died, with Florence using the West 37th Street apartment as her bolt-hole and escape from the constant ringing of the telephone. St. Clair waited until after her death to have a phone installed at number 66.

On the wall of their bedroom in the apartment was a silk tapestry, a heart and a circle of flowers that

Suite 86 of the Hotel Seymour became
Florence's official residence.

represented Romeo and Juliet and that had once been used to decorate the meetings of the Verdi Club. 'We put it over the bed as a symbol of our love,' St. Clair told Betty Moorsteen.[8] He called her Bunny; her pet name for him was Whitey. When they were both in New York the pair dined together daily on the stroke of six o'clock.

Florence's social life revolved around her clubs, and soon after she became a member of the Dickens Fellowship and the Euterpe Club she joined the Pocahontas Memorial Association, the New Yorkers, the Rubenstein Club, the Musicians Club of New York and the New York Mozart Society. Women-only clubs had only existed in the United States since the late 1860s, when they were initially established to help support professional women, and in the ensuing decades thousands of clubs and societies populated by predominantly white middle-class women sprang up across the country. Some of these clubs existed to help improve their community, to raise money for impoverished families and to support hospitals and other charitable causes, and as well as raising money these educated (or self-educated) women met to study, discuss and share their passion for art, literature, drama and music. Florence used her wealth and position to make sure that she filled prominent roles in many of the most influential clubs and societies in New York, and along with the above mentioned these included the New York League of American Penwomen, the Dramatic Arts Society and the National

Society of Patriotic Women of America. She knew everyone and was seen everywhere – often in an outrageously outré dress and enormous hat, such as the 'red and green flowered net over white satin and black net in chrysanthemum design, with gauze brimmed red and black hat and paradise aigrettes' she wore to an equestrian event in 1916.[9]

'Women join and form clubs because they seek social contact with bright and energetic women who know and do things', wrote Kate Louise Roberts in her guide to the intricacies of club life, *The Club Woman's Handybook of Programs and Club Management*. 'It results in relief from housekeeping, from disciplining servants and children and from the narrow mental life which is the routine, everyday experience of the average woman. The social side of club life is to be highly commended and distinctly urged as desirable.'[10]

5 Flo's a Singer

Thanks to a posthumous article in *Coronet* magazine, it has been generally accepted that Florence made her debut as a singer in April 1912[1] – fittingly in the same year that the Titanic sank. Although it would be serendipitous to have these two catastrophic events occurring at the same time, Florence actually first sang in front of an audience at least eighteen months before the world's most iconic ocean liner went down with the loss of almost 1,500 lives. She performed, along with other members of New York's Mozart Society, at a garden party given by President and Mrs. Taft in Washington D.C. in May 1911.[2] Florence's friend Mrs. Noble McConnel (née Wallerstein) founded the Mozart Society in 1909. Dr. Wallerstein had been president of the Rubinstein Club, of which Florence was also a member, but started the Mozart Society – vowing she would make it outshine the Rubinstein – after Mrs. William R. Chapman ousted her from her role in a bloodless coup. As one of over a hundred members of the Mozart Society's choral group, Florence also took part in the December concerts held by the society in the ballroom of the Hotel Astor in both 1910 and 1911.

HOTEL ASTOR
THE GRAND BALL ROOM
CONVENTION HALL OF THE NEW YORK CITY FEDERATION OF WOMEN'S CLUBS

Florence made her first public appearance in New York as a member of the Mozart Society's choral group, at the Hotel Astor in 1910.

Over the next few years Florence kept busy by organising performances – many for charity, some featuring herself – for the Euterpe Club and the many other societies of which she was a member. She proved herself a valuable asset to each of the clubs she belonged to and she was a shrewd promoter. She was a gifted talent spotter and most of her productions made money, much of which would be donated to charity or given as bursaries to up-and-coming musicians. Tens, possibly hundreds, of thousands of dollars were raised by Florence in an almost four-decade clubwoman career, and during her reign as 'chairman of music' membership of the Euterpe Club blossomed.

The musical events she programmed took on Herculean proportions: a charity event Florence organised for the Euterpe Club in March 1913 saw a performance of Mascagni's opera *Cavalleria Rusticana*, a Spanish ballet, carnival-themed tableaux vivants and a cast of 150. She was rewarded for her efforts on behalf of the club when, at a May Day luncheon at the Arrowhead Inn in 1915, she was presented with 'a gold watch bracelet as a token of appreciation of her work in the last year'.[3] Later that same year, at a Yuletide concert given by the National Round Table society, she was honoured when a song, *My Memory Maid*, was dedicated to her by its authors Louise Reichman and Arthur Hintze.[4] She gave her time, and spent a good deal of her money, to encourage young musicians, as the Texan tenor Charles Cameron Bell recalled after he spent part of July 1916 in New York trying to line up work. 'I found her a sympathetic, kindly disposed lady,' he told the *Musical Courier*. 'She was more than generous in her praise of my voice. I sang one day for her in a Carnegie Hall studio. It was a pleasure to tell her of my work and the place that I occupy in San Antonio. She encouraged me to come to New York and said that she would do all in her power to place me well, and that several clubs would hear me gladly whenever I might consent to appear before them.'[5] A decade or so later another musician from San

Antonio would come in to her life and have his own destiny inextricably linked with hers.

In 1917, after much encouragement from friends, who convinced her that she could do so much for music in New York, Florence founded her own musical society, the Verdi Club. Although she had initially resisted the idea of fronting her own organisation, worried it seems about the number of people who would join, the club – which she dedicated to advancing the careers of American artists and musicians – was an instant success and she installed herself as both president and musical director. 'During the season three musical mornings, two musical and dramatic afternoons and a song recital will be given by the club at the Waldorf-Astoria, the programmes being interpreted by prominent artists. In the winter a musicale and reception will be given at the Astor Hotel and a piano recital at Aeolian Hall, the events of the winter being concluded by a dance in April,' the *New York Herald* announced that November, when reporting on the club's debut.[6] She would finance their annual Ball of the Silver Skylarks until she died, and often appeared in the club's tableaux vivants – elaborate still life 'living pictures' with members of the club appearing in extravagant costumes as figures from history, literature or art. Florence was adamant that her new club would do more than just honour the memory of Giuseppe Verdi: the world was at war, and the women of the Verdi Club wanted to contribute to the war effort.

Florence made several appearances as Wagner's Brünn-hilde, the first in March 1915.

The entire proceeds from the club's events were donated to the Red Cross.

The reputation of the Verdi Club's opulent functions spread quickly, along with the fame of the society's founder and president. The club sponsored its own string trio and quartet, and would regularly put on entire operas, in costume and with full sets. It is said that she spent around $2,000 a year out of her own pocket to support the club's lofty aims, and – despite modestly telling a reporter from the *Musical Courier* that 'I think two or three people may be there' for the club's Members Day in February 1920[7] – by the start of that year membership had swelled to over five hundred. By 1934 that figure had become eight hundred.

Florence certainly knew the right people: she had already made the acquaintance of the great Polish pianist and composer Ignacy Jan Paderewski, the world's greatest tenor Enrico Caruso, members of foreign royalty and many other notables of the day, from displaced Russian princes to the niece of the German president, Baroness von Hindenburg. This was a time of profound change in America: the First World War ended, the economy began to boom, women finally got the vote and – with the promise of prosperity, more leisure time and the great technological advances that characterised the Roaring Twenties – more and more people relocated from rural areas to the country's large cities. Florence was soon rubbing shoulders with Vanderbilts and Astors and all manner of well-to-do women. St. Clair kept busy too, appearing in several shows, looking after Florence's nascent career and helping to establish the Actors' Equity Association (the American actors' union). After a lean period during the war – St. Clair wrote (in *The Stage Yearbook,* 1919) that 'touring companies have been entirely shut off from portions of the States owing to the war' and that 'a great number of legitimate houses in the smaller towns were converted into movie houses because the theatres were unable to obtain plays' – things were picking up for him. He joined veteran actor George Arliss's company (Florence was friends with Mrs. Arliss, who was also called Florence, and Mr. and Mrs. Arliss were also members of the Verdi Club) and was often on tour, away from the bright lights of New York and from his beloved Bunny. When he was performing in New York Florence would usually be seen at opening night, and she often sent him good luck telegrams when he was appearing outside the city.

Although she may have dreamed of singing Tosca from beneath the proscenium arch of New York's Metropolitan Opera, the Verdi Club gave her the perfect platform for her performances and plenty of opportunity for her to indulge in her eccentricities. Florence was well liked by her fellow members and, although the club could (and did) regularly attract top talent – such as the mezzo-soprano Grace Hoffman – they would encourage their president to take part. Florence could often be heard tinkling the ivories for the many visiting singers, and on occasion she would sing a duet with one of their guests. During December 1919, when the Verdi Club, along with several other musical societies, was enlisted to provide entertainment at Playland, a Christmas carnival held in New York's Grand Central Palace exhibition hall, Florence took to the stage for an hour and played piano for cellist Marbella Armand, pianist Marie Lohman, tenor Ronald Allan and the soprano Thelma Thelmaire. Two weeks later she played piano again for Mr. Allan and Miss Armand, this time at the McAlpin Hotel for a function organised by the National Patriotic Society, that mysterious arm injury not causing her too many issues, it seemed.

Each spring the Verdi Club would host their magnificent Ball of the Silver Skylarks. The grand ballroom of the Waldorf-Astoria Hotel was taken over by Florence and her team of willing clubwomen, and the events would attract a ticket-paying audience of up to a thousand. 1920 saw the Verdi Club host an Arabian Nights-themed pageant at the ball, preceded by an almost complete performance of the Friedrich von Flotow opera *Martha*. That night Florence appeared as Scheherazade, accompanied by the composer Arthur Gollnik as her sultan; Gollnik later wrote a song, *Dreamy Eyes,* which he dedicated to the club.

'The entrance of President Jenkins was the signal for an outburst of applause,' reported the *Musical Courier*, 'for this lady has endeared herself to all who know her. Her costume was of brilliant white, with rhinestones a glare of dazzling shimmer.'[8] At the following year's event, 'expressing the affection that members feel for their genial founder and president', Florence was presented with a heart-shaped pearl pendant with a large ruby at its centre.[9] Florence's fellow clubwomen often bestowed expensive gifts on their president: over the years she was given several diamond-encrusted watches, bracelets, luxurious handbags and on one occasion, according to a report in the The Sun (New York), 'a golden laurel wreath surrounding a lyre of gold to which was attached an enamelled shield of red and gray, the colors of the club'.[10] Again she saw to it that these functions would raise money for good causes, and her dedication was rewarded when the Italian Red Cross presented her with a gold medal for her largesse. St. Clair also bought her jewellery: for their twenty-fifth wedding anniversary in 1934 he gave her a silver necklace.

In November 1922 a performance was given by Florence at the Verdi Club that set the tone for years to come. That recital was 'so vociferously and continuously applauded that she had to add encores. So many flowers were handed her that it took several ushers to handle them and an extra taxicab to carry them to her salons, which afterward took on the appearance of a bower of chrysanthemums and roses. Many friends wired her, sent her letters and called her the next day on the telephone, one of these poetic admirers wiring: "Heaven gave you a silver throat, and blessed you with golden tones."'[11] The following year, to mark Verdi's birthday, the club purchased two blue spruce trees a full twelve feet high, which Florence had planted on either side of the statue of Verdi which still stands in a small park at the intersection of 72nd Street and Broadway, now known as Verdi Square. 'Mrs. Jenkins rented a portable organ and took her accompanist and me to [the] park. There she planted the trees on behalf of the Verdi Club. Then I played the obbligato while she sang – and shrieked – Joyce Kilmer's "Trees" to the amazement of passers-by,' recalled Mozelle Bennett Sawyer.[12] According to a report that appeared in the *Amsterdam Evening Recorder,* Florence was not the only person to sing that day, although the journalist downplayed Madame's unique contribution: 'Commander Adams of the United States Navy made the presentation speech and Park Commissioner Gallatin accepted the trees on behalf of the city. The Italian consul gave the address. The exercises were opened by the singing of The Star Spangled Banner and closed with the Italian national anthem. Following the presentation speech Miss Grace Marcella Liddane, Amsterdam's gifted soprano, sang Joyce Kilmer's beautiful poem, Trees. Her rendition was so effective that she was requested to repeat the song. She was accompanied by Miss Moselle [sic] Bennett. Mrs. Florence Foster Jenkins, president of the Verdi

Club, had a prominent part in the ceremonies, which were attended by a distinguished audience.'[13]

The autumn, winter and spring months were busy for Florence, whose diary was packed with salons, soirees and other musical events. The Verdi Club itself hosted eleven events a year, from luncheons and musical mornings to its famed annual ball, and these events would attract the cognoscenti of the day: the great Italian conductor Arturo Toscanini attended the unveiling of a bust of Verdi (sculpted by Florence Darnault, which was commissioned by Florence but, according to Darnault, never paid for) in 1934; the club already owned at least one other bust of Verdi, sculpted by Lily Mayer in 1921. The club gave regular Shakespearian matinees, with St. Clair adapting some of the playwright's best known works: 'The interest of the club in the immortal bard is based upon the Verdi utilization of the Shakespearian play for his libretti, as witness his "Othello", "Falstaff" and "Macbeth" as operatic way marks. These performances are directed by St. Clair Bayfield, of the Belasco forces and at present appearing in "Deburau". The cast for these special performances, in aid of the Italian Red Cross, is drawn from the players in current successes.'[14]

As if that wasn't enough to keep her occupied, she also joined a group of thirty clubwomen and socialites in organising, funding (to the tune of $100,000) and directing New York's Beethoven Symphony Orchestra.[15] She

Florence with one of her many feathered fans, circa 1920.

left the city during the summer, regularly taking up residence in Larchmont Manor, Long Island. During these extended absences she kept up her society duties, entertaining members of the Verdi Club at her holiday home and at the nearby Horseshoe Harbor Club, one of the oldest yacht clubs in the United States, of which, naturally, she was a member. She would often travel to Saratoga Springs, was a regular at horse shows in New Jersey and each year would visit Newport, Rhode Island where she would also give an annual charity recital. St. Clair would often accompany Florence on these trips, but they would always stay in separate hotels: Florence with her society friends in the best suites, St. Clair in much more modest lodgings.

In 1928 she met the pianist and conductor Edwin McArthur. She was impressed by his performance at a musical evening at the Barbizon, a hotel on the corner of Lexington Avenue and 63rd Street and at that time used exclusively by young women, and she invited him to come for an interview. He went to her official residence at the Hotel Seymour. 'Her suite was filled with an assortment of bric-a-brac such as you've never seen,' he told *Opera News* in 1963. 'Pictures of herself in various poses, statuettes, lamps of all description, photographs of artists she knew. And she knew everybody.' Born in Denver in September 1907, McArthur began playing the piano professionally while he was still in his teens, moving to New York to study at the Juilliard School

Edwin McArthur, Florence's regular accompanist from
1928 to 1933.

– then, as now, regarded as one of the world's leading
music schools – and to work as an organist, vocal coach
and piano teacher.

McArthur was offered, and accepted, the role of her
regular accompanist. He would play for Florence for
the next five years. Around this time Florence began

to host a series of musical soirees at her suite in the Hotel Seymour. These elite Wednesday evening gatherings would feature dramatic recitations, performances by guest musicians and singers, and often – but not always – Florence herself would perform, in costume, accompanied by McArthur or another pianist if he was not available. Only close friends, musicians and people of influence were lucky enough to be invited to these select gatherings, such as the caricaturist Al Hirschfeld and the famed photographer Margaret Bourke White, who attended a Seymour suite soiree one night in 1937, taking dozens of photographs of Madame and her guests for a *Life* magazine article, 'Life Goes to a Party'. Unfortunately the article never appeared in print.

6 I Hope the Boat Sinks!

The end of the 1920s and the dawn of the new decade was a turbulent time. Black Tuesday – 29 October 1929 – saw the biggest financial crash in American history, the stock market losing between $8 billion and $9 billion in value. The crash, coming just over a month after the London Stock Exchange had collapsed, signalled the beginning of a decade-long Great Depression that affected every industrialised country in the Western world. In the United States unemployment rose and wages fell, and in the cities thousands of businesses failed. In rural communities across the country farmers lost their land and hundreds of thousands of people were made homeless. By 1932 the unemployment rate in the US had soared past 20 per cent, and thousands were forced to live in crudely built shantytowns, scraping a meagre, miserable existence. The Roaring Twenties were well and truly over.

The hardships suffered by others at this time had little effect on Florence. As sole heir to the Foster fortune her mother's death in 1930 gave her even more money and yet more opportunity to pursue her dreams of a career on stage. Mary's obituary, which appeared in the

8 November edition of the *New York Times,* stated that she was 'a member of 42 clubs and societies, including many patriotic organisations. She belonged to the Society of the Daughters of Holland Dames of New York and the Society of Virginia Antiquities, and held life memberships in the National Society of Patriotic Women, Huguenot Society and Easter Star. For 15 years she had been a delegate to the Daughters of the American Revolution congress in Washington.' Three years before her death Mary had arranged for the restoration of Castle Fleming (now known as the Samuel Fleming House), a historic home built in New Jersey in 1756, which she donated to the Daughters of the American Revolution who maintained it as its headquarters and museum until 2005. A plaque unveiled at the dedication of the restored house read 'Presented to Colonel Lowrey Chapter by Mrs. Charles D. Foster, a granddaughter of Judge Andrew Hoagland a Slave-holder whose pocket-book was ever ready to assist others.'

It has been said that, because of her mother's disapproval, Florence did not give full rein to her calling until after Mary died, but this is simply not true. As early as 1916 Mary Foster was hosting events featuring performances by her daughter. Florence was sixty-two when Mary died at her suite at the Park Central Hotel, which, rather fittingly, was situated directly opposite Carnegie Hall. At an age when most people are thinking about retiring, she was readying to launch herself on to the world stage, yet although she was praised for her diction and interpretation of her chosen material the truth is that if she ever hit a correct note during her career it was more by accident than design. 'I do think that she could not hear her own work in the proper pitch,' Cosme McMoon once revealed. 'That's one of the characteristics of her singing.'

In spite of this, some would say because of this, she became tremendously popular. Audiences adored her for the amusement she provided, her stoicism in the face of failure and her staunch belief that she was indeed as great as her contemporaries – if not greater. Cole Porter is said to have written a song for her, although if he did she does not appear to have ever performed it. He rarely missed a performance however – Claude Henry Neuffer wrote that listening to Madame perform *Adele's Laughing Song* caused him 'to laugh so hard [that] he toppled [from] his chair'[1] – and he was a huge fan of her highly camp, exuberant style. Helen Hokinson, the famed *New Yorker Magazine* cartoonist, was an ardent admirer, and Florence and her fellow clubwomen inspired many of her greatest caricatures. The conductor Sir Thomas Beecham chose her version of *Adele's Laughing Song* as one of his favourite recordings for the BBC radio programme *Desert Island Discs*, and it has been reported that Caruso was a fan: although the world's greatest tenor died in 1921, years before her greatest triumphs, he was an honorary member of the Verdi Club and chair of its Advisory Board. As well as donating gifts to the club including, in March 1919, a signed photograph which Florence had copied and given to members of the club, he is reputed to have heard Florence sing and to have confessed that he had never heard anything like it. She compared herself to the renowned sopranos of the day, including Luisa Tetrazzini who, prior to her death in 1940, was considered by many to be the queen of coloratura singing, and she dismissed the laughter that often accompanied her performances as coming from 'hoodlums' planted in the audience by her 'spiteful enemies'.[2] With her enormous ego, she simply attributed such boorish behaviour to professional jealousy.

Surrounded by flowers, believing that the sweet-smelling bouquet could only enhance both her performance and the enjoyment of her audience, she struggled to hit her notes, often leaving an awkward silence as her vocal cords strained to reach the higher register. Ignorant of her limitations and buoyed by her supporters, she blithely carried on. It's true that, as one reporter put it, she was 'wealthy enough to indulge herself in her amateur career, and cheered on by a group of faithful sycophants,'[3] but she was no fool: 'Some may say that I couldn't sing, but no one can say that I didn't sing,' she once confided to a friend.[4] The fact that we're still marvelling at her career when the vast majority of her contemporaries have been all but forgotten proves her right.

A cartoon of Florence and Cosme which appeared in the *American Weekly,* 1944.

At a tea party in 1932, St. Clair Bayfield met an attractive and headstrong young piano teacher by the name of Kathleen Weatherly. He and Miss Weatherly began an affair that would continue for the rest of Florence's life and, according to Kathleen (who was known to her friends as Kay), Florence was not entirely unaware of the situation: 'He told a member of the Verdi Club that his English friend was joining up for the war in 1942. When he said, well, he expected every loyal Englishman would want to do that, Florence replied "It isn't a man, it's a woman. And I hope the boat sinks!"' One weekend, around the Fourth of July, Florence arrived unexpectedly at the West 37th Street apartment. 'He had no phone but messages from his club would be phoned to Florence's apartment and an urgent one came that weekend,' Kay revealed. 'Suddenly the doorbell rang at 7am – he knew instinctively what it was. He told me to get into the closet: it was all jumbled up with Verdi Club theatricals. He pressed the buzzer and Florence arrived in his room with a message that he must go to the Bucks County Theatre in New Hope, Pennsylvania to be on rehearsal. As she came in he suddenly spied my very pretty green leather mules under the bed, but he stood in front of them. She only visited for about five minutes, [but] it was the worst [thing] I've ever experienced. For him it would have been agony if she had found out, though he always said she was psychic.' St. Clair was not the only one to be swayed by the attentions of other suitors: as late as 1943 columnist Danton Walker was reporting on an 'autumnal romance between Prince Galitzin, scion of a noble Russian family, and Florence Foster Jenkins, the veteran Cantatrice whose annual concerts at the Ritz have been the musical sensation of every season for two or three decades'.[5]

In a 2006 interview conducted by Gregor Benko while researching Florence's life for the documentary *A World of Her Own,* pianist Bill Brady, a friend of Kay Bayfield, revealed that 'Bayfield was attracted to domineering women and he and Florence were in love for some years. But by the time Kay appeared on the scene their love affair had cooled considerably: they were companions and associates, but not really lovers. In Kay, St. Clair met someone who was even more domineering and controlling that Florence. After they became secret lovers, Kay agitated for him to separate himself from Florence and he tried, but he was too weak. Florence would not allow him to drop out of her life and insisted that he continue to function as her escort, artistic director etcetera.' Adolf Pollitz, who appeared with Madame in tableaux for the Verdi Club (once famously as Stephen Foster to her Angel of Inspiration), revealed to Brady that he was certain that Florence knew that St. Clair and Kay were having an affair behind her back, but that she never spoke about it to anyone in her circle; she seemed content to continue to support Bayfield so long as her name was not associated with a scandal – a trait Florence inherited from her parents. 'I knew that if anything happened he would desert me at once,' Kay admitted. 'He was absolutely tied to her by an umbilical cord.'

Only once did St. Clair risk breaking that bond, inviting Kay to the Verdi Club's annual Ball of the

Silver Skylarks in 1940. 'I was to bring officers from the British merchant navy,' Kay revealed. 'He said I should be lost amongst the crowd and not observed and he could dance with me. I had on a lovely white ball gown with a peculiar velvet sash and he looked ravishing in his tails. I was sitting on a side table and beckoned him as he came round. Somehow or other we missed; he didn't hear me call out as he passed and he didn't notice me. He had so much on his mind, naturally anxious that the ball should go well. I was so timid and also scared of anything going wrong that I should have been noticed. I would have loved to dance with St. Clair at the Plaza ballroom. He often talked of it after and he felt the sadness of it really acutely.'

7 Meet Mr. McMoon

Although she may have been stunningly inept as a singer, Florence's vast fortune made it possible for her to rent out the Grand Ballroom of the Ritz-Carlton Hotel to host a celebrated annual evening of musical entertainment each autumn. As *Time* magazine put it on 19 November 1934, 'Mrs. Jenkins is well able to pay for a hall. Last week she hired the ballroom of the Ritz-Carlton Hotel and smartly-dressed New Yorkers fairly fought for tickets to get in.' 'She used to give her biggest affair every year at the Ritz-Carlton Hotel,' St. Clair told *PM Daily*.[1] 'The room would be packed to the doors, 800 people, an enormous crush. It got bigger and bigger every year.' Each recital would be accompanied by an opulent printed programme, in red ink on silver paper or, for Hallowe'en, orange on black.

Would-be concertgoers would have to call on her in person to purchase a ticket (and partake of a small glass of sherry and perhaps a slice of cake with Madame), and newspaper reporters were refused entrance. 'I'm putting you down rather near to the front,' she would tell people. 'There's always so much noise farther back.'[2] Her small but loyal entourage of hangers-on and eccentrics would gladly fill those front seats as she took to the stage even though, as the writer Simon Doonan put it, she sounded 'like a turkey being gang-raped'.[3] Those intent on enjoying the burlesque would occupy the rows at the back of the auditorium, where they could laugh without being seen or could make a quick exit if they were overcome with mirth.

Perhaps unsurprisingly she attracted a large following from New York's gay scene, drawn to the pantomime quality of her performances and the sheer extravagance of her outrageous costumes and sets, as Paul Moor put it in his 1963 *Harper's* magazine article 'Roses for Lady Florence': 'one could not escape noticing the exceptionally high percentage of obvious homosexuals, both male and female, who had apparently come to have a laugh at another manifestation of nature's sense of caprice'.[4] Dressed in her favourite Angel of Inspiration costume she wheezed and warbled her way through songs by Brahms, Strauss, Verdi and Mozart. The audience, many there by invitation only, would stuff their fists or their handkerchiefs into their mouths to suppress their laughter: Florence is said to have mistaken their bulging cheeks for evidence of their enjoyment. She created her infamous attire herself, inspired by the Howard Chandler Christy painting, *Stephen Foster and the Angel of Inspiration*: a satin gown with a pair of feathered wings, topped with a tiara and a tinsel halo held in place with a stick that

Florence's most famous costume, the Angel of Inspiration.

made the rather well-built chanteuse resemble an over-fed pet goose.

Among the people who fought to get a ticket to her Ritz-Carlton performances was one George Marek, who would go on to work for RCA Records and who would champion the issue of Madame's 1954 album *A Florence! Foster!! Jenkins!! Recital!!!* The son of a Viennese dentist, as a child he frequented the city's State Opera House. When he was seventeen his family sent him to the United States, where one of his first jobs was in the ostrich-feather department of a milliner's establishment in New York – quite possibly the same store that supplied Madame with the plumage for her outrageous costumes.

The 1934 *Time* article continued:

Mrs. Jenkins appeared in flame-colored velvet, with yellow ringlets piled high on her head. For a starter she picked Brahms' *Die Mainacht*, subtitled on her gilt program as 'O singer, if thou canst not dream, leave this song unsung'. Mrs. Jenkins could dream if she could not sing. With her hands clasped to her heart she passed on to *Vergebliches Standchen*, which she had labeled 'The Serenade in Vain.'

The audience, as Mrs. Jenkins' audiences invariably do, behaved very badly. In the back of the hall men and women in full evening dress made no attempt to control their laughter. Dignified gentlemen sat with hand-kerchiefs stuffed in their mouths and tears of mirth streaming down their cheeks. But Mrs. Jenkins went bravely on. For a Spanish group she wore a mantilla, carried a big feather fan [and] undertook a few little dancing steps to convey more spirit. While she was getting her breath, the Pascarella chamber group played Dvorak's Quintet and cameramen photographed the happy laughing faces in the audience.

Mrs. Jenkins' voice was a little tired but back she came in blue and cream satin, a rhinestone stomacher and a rhinestone tiara. Cinemen turned their cameras on her while she struggled with the *Vissi d'Arte* from Tosca. Last year she sang a flower song while tossing roses into the audience. In her excitement the basket slipped from her hand, hit an old gentleman on the head. Last week she repeated the flower song, pleased her friends by again hurling the basket.

After 'The Ant and the Grasshopper' and an arrangement of the 'Blue Danube' made by her friend, Cosme McMoon, Mrs. Jenkins was too exhausted for encores. Flushed and happy, surrounded by flowers, she made a little speech in which she asked members of the audience to write and tell her which songs they had liked the best. Said she: 'It may not be important to you, but it is very important to me. Next week I am singing in Ithaca.'

It's fascinating to think that, if the reviewer is to be believed, film footage exists of this performance. Sadly, nothing has surfaced to date. A film of Florence in full flight was made of her Ritz-Carlton recital in October

1935 and was screened at least once, on 13 December that year, at a Verdi Club musical and dramatic afternoon (where St. Clair also presented a one-act version of the play *Mary, Queen of Scots*), but that too has been lost.

'It is too bad,' wrote Francis Robinson, Assistant Manager of the Metropolitan Opera, that 'she did not record her favourite encore, *Clavelitos*, a number she invariably had to repeat.'[5] As reported in *Time*, it is an accepted part of her legend that, on at least one occasion, the basket followed the flowers into the audience (in 1942 *Time* again wrote that 'Her specialty [is] a flower song in which she massively hurls flowers, basket and all, at the heads of her following'). Contemporary accounts describe how Florence appeared on stage resplendent in a Spanish shawl and mantilla with a jewelled comb and, like Carmen, a red bloom in her hair, punctuating her performance of the song by tossing flowers variously described as carnations or roses from her basket to her delighted audience. Before Madame could return to the stage for her encore her overworked but unflinchingly loyal accompanist Cosme McMoon and two uniformed ushers 'had to pass among the jubilant groundlings and retrieve the prop buds and basket. The enthusiasm of the audience at this point reached a peak that beggars description.'[6]

Described by the *San Antonio Evening News* as having 'real talent and, in addition, a pleasing stage appearance',[7] McMoon had joined her happy throng in 1930, having previously been accompanist for the contralto Elsie Baker. Cosme initially played alongside Edwin McArthur but replaced him permanently after a recital at the Ritz-Carlton, presumably in 1933 (McArthur played for the Verdi Club in March 1933, so he cannot have upset Florence prior to this). While Madame was performing an aria from *Faust*, in full costume as usual, laughter could be heard, which she accused McArthur of causing by pulling faces. 'The way the lights flared up, she said it made him look like a hemogoblin [sic],' Adolf Pollitz revealed, 'and the audience laughed. He got a laugh and repeated it.'[8] After the performance McArthur turned to her and is reported to have said: 'I suppose you won't have anything to do with me now,' to which Florence replied: 'I certainly will not!'[9] McArthur would go on to become the regular accompanist for the noted Norwegian soprano Kirsten Flagstad, accompanying her in more than a thousand concerts. In a widely respected career that spanned some sixty years, Edwin McArthur was the music director of the St. Louis Municipal Opera, the conductor of the Harrisburg Symphony and the director of the Opera Department of the Eastman School of Music, but from that point on he would never play for Florence again: Cosme McMoon became her preferred pianist.

He was born Cosme McMunn in Durango, Mexico in 1901, one of six children; his father, also called Cosme, had been born in Mexico to Irish immigrant parents.

Cosme McMoon, Florence's loyal accompanist, in 1937.

The McMunns were forced to leave their home in 1911 during the Mexican revolution, settling in San Antonio, Texas. Like Florence, Cosme junior was a child prodigy: 'His older cousin Manuela McMunn was his first piano teacher,' his nephew Mark explains. 'But by the time Cosme was ten there was nothing else she could teach him, and Manuela was a very fine pianist. There are other musicians in the family but none anywhere near Cosme's calibre. The man was a true piano virtuoso and composer.'

After he had exhausted what resources were available to him locally, Cosme would go on to study in Europe. He appears to have altered his name to match its Mexican pronunciation sometime around 1918: in February 1919, as Cosme McMoon, he copyrighted his own composition *Sondes de la Fete*, and in 1920 he moved to New York. Cosme gave his first public recital in the metropolis at the Plaza Hotel in 1922. Lauded by the *New York Times* for 'the agility of his fingers and the clarity of his technique',[10] before he began playing for Florence he had himself appeared as a concert pianist, composed and copyrighted several original pieces and even co-written a play (*Cleo*, described as 'a farce in three acts') in 1925. He did not think she had great talent, believing that she could not hear her own voice properly, but he admired her spirit and her passion for music, and he was happy to play for her. Over more than a decade together he would help her put together her programmes and attempt to coach her singing. Her generosity afforded him financial independence, and after he became Madame's regular accompanist Cosme would continue to perform solo recitals, teach and compose for others – the pianist Florence Mercuro played three of his songs at a recital at the Carnegie Chamber Music Hall in April 1940 – as long as his commitments to Florence allowed him time to do so. Described as 'an unexpectedly young, nice-looking man who may well have no parallel in history when it comes to control of the facial muscles,' by Paul Moor, he 'afforded her heroic assistance. A light, pleasant smile on his face at all times, no matter what new surprises she came up with, he was always right there with her.'[11] On the rare occasion when Cosme was unavailable, Florence would use organist and choir director William J. Cowdrey, who appeared with her at several of her Newport recitals, or other piano players to accompany her.

'I remember her when she sang *Aida*,' Florence Darnault recalled. 'She came out in costume. She had all these harem women, and had all the other faces darkened, but she didn't darken hers. These women were all dark, none of them sang, they couldn't sing a note. They were from the Verdi Club; they were all big women and they all had these chiffon trousers . . . I think that was the worst I ever saw.'

The question has to be asked: if she was indeed so bad, how did she manage to lead such an active career, and how was it that she was complimented in print as 'holding the wonder of the audience' and having a 'remarkable voice'?[12] So great was her following that she was booked by a local radio station WINS to broadcast every Sunday for five months (May-September) during 1938[13] and she appeared throughout the 1930s and early 40s in concerts in New England, Washington (where, wrote critic Dr. B.B. James, quoted in an advertisement in the *Musical Courier*, 'the capacity audience included persons from the political, cultural and intellectual society'[14]), Philadelphia, Saratoga Springs and Newport, Rhode Island. The vast majority of her notices – and there are many, many mentions of Florence's performances in contemporary newspapers and magazines – are respectful and gentle: many could be called glowing. The *Time* article of 1934, quoted above, is the first real criticism of her, and even then the

Florence photographed al fresco, at the
Biltmore Club, Westchester, October 1938.

reviewer singles out the audience rather than Madame as
being the problem. A review of her annual Ritz-Carlton
recital in 1935 talks of her 'exuberant style' and states
that 'the wildly applauding audience left no doubt of the
enjoyment derived by the throng'.[15]

There's the occasional satiric turn of phrase, a certain tongue-in-cheek quality to a number of her reviews, but they are overwhelmingly kind and, on the whole, positive. After a concert she gave in August 1922 the conductor Salvatore Paciavalle wrote to her, saying that 'your singing was much enjoyed. The aria from Gioconda was delivered with sincere dramatic feeling, and the waltz-song rang with brilliancy, your tones being beautiful and clear'.[16] Yet today her reputation rests entirely on her final live performance and her handful of recordings, all made at the end of her career when, in her seventies, her voice would have been well past its prime and she may also have been suffering from a lifetime of mercury poisoning. Many people who saw her perform attest to her awfulness, but almost all of these comments came after she made her recording debut, or after she was no longer around to contradict them.

There's a very simple reason for this: Florence was well connected and well liked. She was friendly with the editors and publisher of the *Musical Courier,* the magazine that featured her regularly and was always effusive about her performances (she may well have paid for her reviews to appear in print there) and her charm won over many other would-be critics. Florence had a reputation for never saying an unkind word about anyone – at least not in public. 'She was not catty,' Florence Darnault said. 'She never said a mean thing. I never heard her say a mean thing about a human being.' Keeping newspaper and magazine reporters at bay and only selling tickets to her recitals by word of mouth kept up her mystique and added to the 'in crowd' feel experienced by her listeners: it seems that once she allowed the general public to hear her, however, the gloves were off.

'I can remember one evening when she wore a Spanish costume and sang an aria from Carmen," wrote violinist Mozelle Bennett Sawyer, whom Florence engaged on several occasions. 'As usual, she was slightly off-key and substituted shrieks for some of the high notes. Because she was plump and awkward, and very serious about what she was doing, we were always on the verge of hysteria – especially when, as Carmen, she threw a rose at the audience. Everyone wanted to get invited to the Verdi Club because it was such fun to try and keep from laughing."[17] 'Some of her admirers of long standing say the lady is quite deaf,' wrote Richard S. Davis. 'They say she mistakes the groundswell as surging applause."[18] One thing is certain, that whatever her limitations as a singer she was adored by her friends. In 1938, as a mark of their respect, the members of the Verdi Club commissioned a bust of Florence from the Hungarian sculptor Baroness Liane de Gidro, who had previously sculpted Caruso, Liszt, General Pershing and Mussolini.

8 Madame Makes a Record

Performing in front of a rapturous, handpicked audience instilled in Florence the unshakable conviction that she was indeed a diva to be reckoned with. Now she was ready to foist her gift on the wider world, and to preserve evidence of her vocal prowess for the ages.

Florence's recordings were all made at the Melotone Recording Studio, situated in an Art Deco high rise at 25 Central Park West, New York. Fittingly the same company issued the only known recordings by the Boston-born socialite turned horrendous soprano Tryphosa Bates-Batcheller (by strange coincidence in the very same year as Florence made her recording debut). The studio was just a half hour's walk away from the apartment she and St. Clair shared. Not that she walked anywhere: even during the war years and those of the depression if she could not persuade a friend, such as the dutiful Adolf Pollitz, to drive her then she would take taxis everywhere and always tried to get out of paying for them herself. Her sessions (the first took place in May 1941, when she recorded the *Queen of the Night* aria and *The Bell Song* from Delibes' opera *Lakmé*) were self-financed and the early discs

Florence and Cosme's second release, the
infamous *Queen of the Night* recording.

privately pressed in small batches with typewritten
labels.

Her recording of *Der Hölle Rache* (better known as the
Queen of the Night aria) from Mozart's *The Magic Flute*
set the standard for what would follow: it's a chaotic cat-
erwaul, with both piano and voice chasing each other
around the scale as if they were Tom and Jerry fighting
each other over a bowl of milk. It's worth remembering
that she was seventy-three years old before she stepped
into the recording studio and that all of her performances
were captured in one single take. Only her final session
when, in January 1943, she recorded *Biassy* and *Adele's*

Laughing Song, was done with any thought towards the disc-buying market: 'There is no getting by in this life if one is forever to deny the incredible. We, and other dealers who are in the know, have done pretty well with the previous issues of records – privately issued – by Mme. Florence Foster Jenkins. Mme. Jenkins' vocal art is something for which there is no known parallel. Even after one has heard it, he doesn't believe it. The records hitherto issued have been pressings from stampers made from so-called instantaneous recordings,' the record trade journal, *The Bulletin*, reported in January 1943. 'The new offering of Mme. Jenkins' art was made expressly for commercial production. It is mechanically excellent and vocalistically out of this world. Cosme McMoon does his stuff at the piano. The $2.50 this record costs will give you more of a kick than the same amount invested in tequila, vodka, zubrovka or marijuana, and we ain't woofin'!'

'Mme. Jenkins' visits to the studio were a distinct and radical departure from the customary routines of the many artists for whom Melotone has recorded,' wrote Milton Bendiner.[1] 'Rehearsals, the niceties of volume and pitch, considerations of acoustics – all were thrust aside by her with ease and authority. The technicians never ceased to be amazed at her capacity for circumventing the numerous problems and difficulties peculiar to recording. She simply sang; the disc recorded.'

On only one occasion did Florence question her own

performance: on her first visit to the studio she made a test acetate and, upon hearing it played back, announced to Melotone's director, Mera M. Weinstock, that it was 'excellent, virtually beyond improvement', and insisted that all copies should be made from that same test pressing. The following day Florence telephoned Mera Weinstock, having decided that *The Bell Song* should be issued alone. During the previous evening she had been listening to the acetate and was unhappy with a note towards the end of the *Queen of the Night*. 'My dear Madame Jenkins,' Weinstock assured her, 'You need feel no anxiety concerning any *single* note.'[2] The *Queen of the Night* became the A-side of her second release.

Unusually for what was basically a vanity release, the disc was reviewed in *Time* magazine on 16 June 1941:

> An immensely difficult coloratura soprano aria, even for markswomanly singers, is the one in Mozart's *Magic Flute* in which the Queen of the Night declares that she is boiling with fury. Last week a recording of this air, advertised entirely by rumor, enjoyed a lively little sale at Manhattan's Melotone Recording Studio.
>
> It was recorded to sell to her friends at $2.50 a copy – by Mrs. Florence Foster Jenkins, a rich, elderly amateur soprano and musical clubwoman. Mrs. Jenkins' night-queenly swoops and hoots, her wild wallowings in descending trills, her repeated staccato notes like a cuckoo in its cups, are innocently uproarious to hear, almost as much so as the annual song recital which she

gives in Manhattan. For that event, a minor phenom-
enon in U.S. music, knowing Manhattanites fight for
tickets. Mrs. Jenkins is well pleased with the success of
her *Queen of the Night* record, and hopes to make others. Her fans hope so too.

Singer and author Vernon Alfred Howard wrote
that 'the shrieking off pitch high notes, the staggering
roulades slowed to a walk, the wafer-thin timbre, the
breathless attacks, the fractured musical line – all make
us laugh (and cringe) at the sheer awfulness of it all . . .
Jenkins' performances are a catalogue of every vocal
fault and failure imaginable.'[3]

All her recordings are decidedly out of tune but are
equally, utterly mesmerising. *Time* magazine once wrote
of her: 'Critics have long wondered whether Coloratura
Jenkins' art can be described as singing at all. But she
will intrepidly attack any aria, scale its altitudes in great
swoops and hoots, [and] assay its descending trills with
the vigor of a maudlin cuckoo. Her recitals are jam-
packed with cheering devotees.'[4] Milton Bendiner, writing in *Florence Foster Jenkins, An Appreciation*, said that
'Madame Jenkins' rendition of these arias was ever a
wondrous thing to hear. It transcended the feeble limitations of scale, of tone, even of voice.'[5]

The deluded dowager once informed Mera Weinstock
that she had listened to recordings of the *Queen of the
Night* aria by famed sopranos Frieda Hempel and Luisa

Tetrazzini, and that her own rendition was 'beyond doubt the most outstanding of the three'. Carleton Sprague-Smith, reviewing the disc in the October 1941 issue of *Esquire*, disagreed: 'To add spice to your collection, to make you a Ripley, write to Melotone Recording Studios for Florence Foster Jenkins' singing of the dramatic aria of the Queen of the Night. What I might say about it would be libellous, so I won't. You buy it and, if it isn't worth the price of admission, I'll refund your money.'

McMoon composed several pieces for Florence during their time together, and three of his songs – *Like a Bird* (with words by Florence), *Valse Caressante* and *Serenata Mexicana* – were also recorded at these sessions. During soirees held in her cramped suite at the Hotel Seymour she would play one of her recordings alongside versions by other singers and ask her guests to vote for the one that they preferred. 'She would put the *Bell Song* by herself and by Galli-Curci,' Cosme McMoon revealed. 'Then she would hand little ballots out and you were supposed to vote (for) which one was the best.' Invariably her visitors, all loyal and devoted to Florence, would plump for her own recording. When one guest dared to show favour for the version by Amelita Galli-Curci, one of the most popular sopranos of the day, Madame was mortally offended, and gasped: 'How could you mistake that? My tone is so much fuller than that!' One can only imagine how she would have reacted if anyone had had the courage to compare

Galli-Curci's recording of *Clavelitos* with Madame's own show-stopping performance of the song. It must have given her some satisfaction to know that the flautist Louis Alberghini, who accompanies Florence and Cosme on the recordings of *Charmant Oiseau* and *Valse Caressante* and who had appeared with Madame in recital, had also accompanied Galli-Curci.

These discs could only be purchased from Florence, from the Melotone office or from select dealers in New York such as the Gramophone Shop (established in 1928), which described her first release as 'a most unusual record which must be heard to be believed'. The same establishment, describing her recording of *Biassy*, wrote: 'It will probably suffice to say that here is a new Florence Foster Jenkins record. The soprano considers it her best. The recording clearly reproduces all the idiosyncratic touches that have made Mrs. Jenkins' record of one of the Queen of the Night's arias from *Die Zauberflote* a collector's item.' Madame placed an advertisement in her recital programme to promote her second release:

Special Announcement. Following the sell-out of Mme. Jenkins' record of *Lakme*, there have been innumerable requests for another of her recordings. With the intention of fulfilling the popular request, Mme. Jenkins has made a double record. *The Queen of the Night* by Mozart and the *Serenata Mexicana* by McMoon. This souvenir recording may be obtained by mail order to Recordings, Mme. Jenkins, P.O. Box 94,

Times Square Station. Please enclose check with orders. Copies are $2.50 each disc.

'If you listen to those recordings,' triple Oscar-winner Meryl Streep told the *Washington Post* shortly after she was cast to play Florence in the big screen adaptation of her life, 'she was almost good, and then there was a point when she was off. And that is what makes it funny. It was almost there. It doesn't start out badly. It starts out hopefully.'[6] When a fellow clubwoman, meeting Florence for the first time, had the audacity to ask 'You were a singer, weren't you?', Madame replied, indignantly: 'I *am* a singer!'[7]

Paul Moor, then a callow sixteen-year-old selling furniture in a New York department store, recalled discussing her Melotone recordings with Madame:

> 'I've heard some of your records,' I said. She seemed to be waiting, so I added, uncertainly, 'I found them – really extraordinary.'
>
> 'Oh, how kind you are!' She giggled with unaffected pleasure. 'Which records of mine do you know?'
>
> I said the first title that occurred to me: '*Like a Bird I am Singing*'. 'Flatterer!' She laughed gaily. 'You're just saying that because of course you know I wrote the poem! But I do think Mr. McMoon has set it to music really beautifully, and with great sensitivity. I've made quite a number of records, you know. I go to that recording studio there on Central Park West.

Such kind people! At first they seemed surprised that I would simply run through each song or aria a single time when I recorded them, but I feel that if you don't get it right the first time, you won't do it any better the second, so why tire yourself? That's why I don't find recording anywhere near the trial most artists do.'[8]

Florence was exceedingly proud of *Like a Bird*; she had the lyric printed out and sent to her friends as a Christmas card.

Joy of the morning, the river is flowing,
There's a silvery way o'er the crystalline bay.
To the notes of thy flute, the shady groves yearning,
My thoughts of thee bring me, sweet memories thrilling.

Like a Bird I am singing!
Like a Bird on the wing, Like a Bird (ah-ha-ha-ha-ha!)
Like a Bird
(ahhhh-ahhhhhhhh-ahhhhhhh-ah-ha-ha-ha-ha-ha!)

(*Like a Bird*, words by Florence Foster
Jenkins, music by Cosme McMoon)

9 Live at Carnegie Hall

'Madame Jenkins bills herself as a coloratura soprano, which means that she takes the songs that bring out the best in Lily Pons and permits them to bring out her worst. And the worst of Madame Jenkins is something awful.'[1] Bad or not, Florence was venerated by her audience, as Cosme McMoon recalled:

> The audience nearly always tried not to hurt her feelings by outright laughing, so they developed a convention that whenever she came to a particularly excruciating discord or something like that, where they had to laugh, they burst into these salvos of applause and whistles and the noise was so great that they could laugh at liberty.
>
> At that time Frank Sinatra had started to sing and the teenagers used to faint and scream, so she thought she was producing the same kind of effect. When these salvoes of applause came she took them as great marks of approval for her tremendous vocal tour de force ... and she loved that.

A report on her 1935 Ritz-Carlton recital tells us that 'the auditorium held a capacity audience. Including numerous standees, and outbursts of applause punctuated the items presented'.[2] One story, repeated by a United Press reporter in 1954 on the eve of the release of *A Florence! Foster!! Jenkins!!! Recital!!!*, has it that at one performance, when she chose to sing the part of Waldvogel, the wood bird from Wagner's opera *Siegfried*, the young man she had employed to play the title role could not distinguish between Madame's trills and the screeching of a faulty radiator in the auditorium. The recital could not continue until an engineer was located who was able to access the boiler room and sort out the problem. 'The records show that the crowd applauded so hard, Madame Jenkins took 10 curtain calls.'[3]

Robert Coleman, reviewing her penultimate Ritz-Carlton recital for William Randolph Hearst's *New York Daily Mirror*, reported that

> . . . it is possible that pianist McMoon may have been overcome by the enthusiastic roars which greeted Madame's high notes and trills, but he appeared to strum the keys a little too late or too soon on several occasions. And once or twice we failed to hear the piano at all.
>
> Mme. Jenkins' legions of loyal admirers were disconsolate when she failed to make an appearance as 'The Angel of Inspiration'. We suspect that due to the war emergency she was unable to obtain the airplane wire required to support her angelic wings. Mme. Jenkins is incomparable. Her annual recitals bring

unbounded joy to the faded souls of Park Avenue and the musical elite. It is easy to understand, after hearing her, why she's Beatrice Lillie's favorite.[4]

Actress and comedienne Lillie was a gifted parodist: there's no record of her ever having imitated Florence, but Madame would have provided ample material should she have chosen to lampoon her.

Although Florence used much of her vast fortune to further her own career, she was also a great philanthropist, donating her time and money to any number of charities and sponsoring new works by up-and-coming composers. She also penned poems and 'dramatic compositions', several of which were set to music by McMoon, including *Trysting Time*, copyrighted by the pair in August 1933. Unfortunately Cosme does not appear to have written any music for her oddly-titled play *Nye Towitt*, to which Florence registered the copyright in 1940. The music for her 1939 lyric *Trailing Arbutus* was written by Elmo Russ, the author of the song *America Forever Free*. *Trailing Arbutus,* a sentimental song about the passing of her father, was inspired by a gift of the flowers in question from Adolf Pollitz, which he brought from his home in Oyster Bay:

> Now he lies where the daisies lie,
> But, in the springs that are,
> Like the springs that were,
> The scent of Arbutus fills the air.

To my aching heart, it brings a message,
Of hope and joy, to the love that is there.

(*Trailing Arbutus*, words by Florence Foster
Jenkins, music by Elmo Russ)

She was adored by her many friends who found her modest, except for her delusions of musical greatness, kind and endlessly generous; and her soirees were always well attended. When she did charge people to attend her performances prospective audience members had to submit to an interview, as tickets could only be purchased by genuine music lovers. Legend has it that, after an accident in a taxi in 1943, Florence was thrilled to discover that she could sing 'a higher F than ever before'. Instead of suing the taxi company she sent the driver a box of expensive cigars as a thank you. Cosme, it is said, could never find the elusive new note that Madame heard in her head. According to the comedian Alan King she collected chairs that famous people had died in – although King was just sixteen when Florence herself died and it is doubtful that he would have visited her apartment, as Nancy Schimmel points out: 'It seems unlikely that a young person under sixteen would have attended one of Florence's soirees. He doesn't seem like someone Florence would have encouraged. Her focus was on helping musicians rather than comedians.' A story (probably apocryphal) told by *New York Post* correspondent Earl Wilson has it that she was once 'instructed to get some refreshment ready for cameramen coming to call. On the fateful day her adviser (most probably St. Clair) asked if she'd got the "refreshment" and she replied, "Oh yes, I've got it in the bathtub." Elated and hopeful, the adviser went in and looked at the bathtub. It was full of potato salad.'[5]

Paul Moor recalled his visit to Madame's apartment:

> Her manner was bright – almost flirtatious, reminiscent of certain well-born Southern ladies I had known. 'Do sit down – no, there, I think you'll find that more comfortable. That's a man's chair! Will you take tea? Would you prefer a drink? How kind of you to write to me. Do feel free to smoke if you wish.' Her honest hospitableness, plus my awareness of being there under false pretenses, made me feel gauche, but she exercised all the charm at her command to put me at my ease.[6]

Playwright Peter Quilter adapted this same encounter for the opening scene in his Olivier Award-nominated play *Glorious!*

It is said that in her later years she became quite mean with money, and would dress rather dowdily and cheaply when not on stage, even wearing fake furs and trying to pass them off as the real thing. She did not trust banks and, probably as a reaction to her unhappy first marriage, had a deep dislike of doctors – although many of her events raised money for local hospitals and the Italian and American branches of the Red Cross, and she raised funds to pay for an ambulance used at the French front during the war.

On 25 October 1944, at the ripe old age of seventy-six, she performed songs by Mozart, Puccini, McMoon and others, ably supported by Cosme and members of the Pascarella Chamber Music Society, at Carnegie Hall. She was persuaded to take the leap into a public performance by the New York-based promoter George Leyden Colledge and, for the first time in her career, Florence allowed someone other than St. Clair to manage one of her performances. Colledge, whose business was to sponsor New York recitals of leading artists, had a good pedigree (although Kay Bayfield later referred to him disparagingly as 'some card sharper'), having worked for many years for Arthur Judson, the violin prodigy who became a highly successful concert promoter and manager of the New York Philharmonic. He was already known to Florence as he managed the career of Metropolitan Opera contralto Doris Doe, who had appeared before the Verdi Club. George Colledge would later go on to manage the career of contralto Marian Anderson and of coloratura soprano Agata Borzi, and had recently set up his own agency, run from an office in the RKO building (now part of the Rockefeller Center).

Although often cited as her debut, this was not her first performance at the hallowed concert hall: in March 1939 Florence was engaged by the Hungarian Chamber of Commerce to sing Hungarian songs there.[7] She paid

FLORENCE FOSTER
JENKINS
COLORATURA SOPRANO
Assisted by
THE PASCARELLA CHAMBER MUSIC SOCIETY

CARNEGIE HALL
Wednesday Evening, October 25th
At 8:30 o'clock

Florence's final performance took place at the
Carnegie Hall in October 1944.

for the hire of the hall herself (according to *Time* magazine 'Carnegie, on the Philharmonic's off nights, rents
for $400'), and so great was the demand that the con-
cert sold out in just two hours, although there have been
claims that Florence bought most of the tickets herself
and gave them away. A number were certainly given

free to members of the armed forces, via the United Service Organisations for National Defense (USO), which is how the theatre critic Richard Connema, then an eighteen-year-old serving in the United States Army, came to be there: 'I was stationed at Fort Dix and several of us had a weekend pass to go into New York. We went to the Times Square USO to find free tickets to Broadway shows, and there were tickets for the Florence Foster Jenkins concert at Carnegie Hall. I had heard her recordings when I was in high school, she sounded like a cat in heat, but I had never seen her in person. The place was packed.'

Tickets were being scalped for as much as ten times their face value outside, and *Newsweek* reported that two thousand potential purchasers were turned away. 'Carnegie Hall has been completely sold out for the recital to be given there by Florence Foster Jenkins,' the *New York Times* announced.[8] One columnist, Richard S. Davis, suggested that her next concert should be at Madison Square Garden, which had more than six times the capacity of Carnegie Hall.

Performing at Carnegie Hall would fulfil a lifetime's ambition for Madame and, although money was no object, both she and St. Clair knew that she would make a profit on the night: 'Perhaps the only small-time artist who ever breaks even on a Manhattan recital is Philadelphia's Mrs. Florence Foster Jenkins, a clubwoman coloratura now in her 70s,' *Time* magazine had stated two years previously. 'Once a year Singer Jenkins appears on the flower-banked stage of one of Manhattan's smaller auditoriums [and] is always sure of a wildly enthusiastic audience, which comes to be amused. Accompanied by a concert pianist named Cosme McMoon, she does her singing in a variety of flame-colored gowns, stomachers, mantillas, corsages, tiaras, while her yellow curls bob and nod with her vocal vim.'[9] The members of the audience who turned out to see what Madame would wear next would not be disappointed.

The scene he came across that night staggered McMoon: 'When I approached the Hall I could hardly get near it. The crowd stretched all around Seventh Avenue. Inside the house held a record audience; it seemed like the people were hanging off the rafters besides taking up every inch of available room.' Richard Connema agrees: 'Yes, there was a crowd gathering and I remember one person offered to pay triple the amount for our tickets. One of my friends was going to take the money for the ticket but we finally convinced him not to. We arrived about half an hour before the performance and I guess there was a little pandemonium as we entered, however we went inside the Hall without any problems: the people trying to get in were not going to mess with someone in uniform.' Sinatra appeared at Carnegie Hall the same week but had drawn far less of a crowd; however he was speaking in support of Franklin D. Roosevelt's presidential campaign, rather than singing to screaming bobbysoxers. As the *New York Post*'s Harriett Johnson wrote: 'music's topsy-turvey [if] Florence Foster Jenkins can squeak out an aria off key and sell out Carnegie Hall'.[10] Adolf Pollitz took a photograph of the audience from the Carnegie Hall stage: the auditorium is jam-packed with happy faces, all eagerly anticipating an extraordinary night.

The recital began at 8:30 with a trio of English Songs accompanied by Cuban-born flautist Oreste de Sevo. Earl Wilson of the *New York Post* dismissed Madame's performance as 'one of the weirdest mass jokes New York has ever seen'.[11] Richard S. Davis, writing in the *Milwaukee Journal* just two days after the show, described her:

> The mere appearance of the singer provoked a prolonged wave of titters. She was wearing a pale peach gown that was nothing short of a masterpiece. Bright gems glittered on her bosom, around her throat and on her fingers, but the sensation of her costume was an immense fan of orange and white feathers. She waved it coyly at the multitude and laid it on the piano.
>
> And then she sang, or whatever . . .[12]

Madame appeared unwell that evening, and several of the press reports tell of her gripping the piano to steady herself. It could, of course, have been nerves: this was the biggest concert of her career after all, and the audience was peppered with celebrity fans including Cole

Porter (who was witnessed grinding the tip of his cane into his foot to keep himself from laughing), the soprano Lily Pons, burlesque entertainer Gypsy Rose Lee and actress Tallulah Bankhead, who laughed so much that she is reputed to have wet herself and had to be escorted out of the auditorium. The famously hard-drinking and straight-talking Bankhead was a libertine with a deep love of the perverse: just a few years earlier she had been present as Addie (at the age of seventy-nine) and Effie (a mere stripling at sixty-two), two of the notoriously dreadful Cherry Sisters, attempted their penultimate comeback at a nightclub on Broadway.

'At first my friends did not laugh; three of us had heard her recordings and we felt sympathy for her,' admits Richard Connema. 'We were in the orchestra area where officers were but I did hear laughter coming from the audience in the balcony.' Columnist Danton Walker reported that Raymond Scott, the electronic music pioneer, had written a song for her recital, although if he did present Madame with a finished composition she did not perform it on the night.

Anna Russell, the singer and comedienne whose hit album *Anna Russell Sings?* undoubtedly inspired RCA to posthumously release *A Florence! Foster!! Jenkins!!! Recital!!!!*, was there too. 'I was never the same again,' she told Mary Campbell of the Associated Press in 1981. 'I thought "What a good idea. I think I'll have a go at that". So I did.'[13] One critic noted that Florence would have pocketed around $4,000 on the night (equivalent to approximately $54,000 today); he failed to mention that a portion of the profits was donated to wartime charities including the USO and the Army Relief Fund. Pleasingly the programme, which Madame had printed for that evening, is the most requested item in the Carnegie Hall archive. The singer, dancer and Broadway veteran Cris Alexander was there too. 'I went with Gian Carlo Menotti, who was a great fan of hers,' he revealed to Brooks Peters for his 2001 *Opera News* article 'Florence Nightingale'. 'She really was divine. Heavenly. It was one of the funniest nights in the theater. For one number, she came out with a large salad bowl filled with rose petals that she scattered onto the floor. After the song was over she got down on her honkers, scooped them all up and did the entire number over again. It was one of the highlights of my entire theatrical life.'

'I remember that about when she did *Clavelitos,* in *that* outfit, programs were thrown from the balcony down on our heads,' adds Richard Connema. 'I remember some of the officers looked up there to see if there were servicemen among them. She actually thought that she was doing a wonderful job, however during *Clavelitos* she began not to enjoy herself. She appeared shocked but she kept going.'

'I sat in row T, and around me I heard people saying "Shhh, don't laugh so loud; stick something in your mouth . . .",' wrote Earl Wilson.[14] '"We're jackasses for coming ...", "She didn't hit three notes in that one ...". I asked her personal representative, Sinclair Bayfield [sic], "Why?" "She loves music," he said. "If she loves music, why does she do this?" I asked.'

The publicist Alix B. Williamson, who managed the career of the Von Trapp Family Singers for more than two decades, was also in the audience that night. 'I went to several of her concerts,' she told Brooks Peters. 'It was unbelievable, let's put it that way. Jenkins had no voice of any kind. She was a large, big-busted lady. Everyone would laugh out loud when she sang. She would go to change her costumes and say to the audience, "Now don't go away." Then she would reappear in her Angel of Inspiration costume or come out trilling *Like a Bird*!'[15]

'She came out in a shepherdess' gown with a shepherd's crook. The ruckus was so great that it lasted five minutes before there was enough quiet for her to begin,' recalled McMoon. '*Adele's Laughing Song* was especially noteworthy. For this Madame came out in a pastel-coloured gown; her eyes were veritable caverns of mascara with black patches on her face and her head piled up high with yellow ringlets – her favourite wig.' Proceedings ground to a halt at one point: one of her wings became loose and Cosme had to stop playing and help reattach the offending appendage. For his troubles Madame presented her harried accompanist with a solid gold medal – presumably for courage.

'Old admirers of Mme. Jenkins agreed that even she had never been in such voice – or lack of it – and that she had never delivered her florid airs with quite so many misses in form and pitch,' wrote Davis.[16] During the performance, McMoon remembered: 'She put her hands rakishly to her hips and went into a circular dance which was the most ludicrous thing I have ever seen, and created a pandemonium in the place but she was very well satisfied with it. As well she might have been; there was never such enthusiasm or applause or noise heard at Carnegie Hall.' Henry Simon, writing in New York's *PM Daily* newspaper, berated the audience: 'Mrs. Jenkins, who started singing in public comparatively late in life, has been giving recitals in hotels for the past few years, and her performances have developed quite a large following. She now possesses only a pitiful remnant of vocal equipment. The audience, a very large one, punctured the sounds she made with uncontrollable waves of laughter and applauded at the end of each of the three numbers I heard as though they had discovered a new Flagstad. It was the cruellest and least civilized behavior I have ever witnessed in Carnegie Hall, but Mrs. Jenkins met it all with pleased smiles. She was giving the herd pleasure.'[17] Isabel Morse Jones, writing in the *LA Times*, described what she saw: 'I watched this indefatigable old lady, decked out in pink brocade and ostrich plumes. She was barely able to make it across the stage but once she was there she launched into the most

Florence in her Spanish costume, which she
wore to perform her favourite encore, *Clavelitos*.

pathetic exhibition of vanity I have ever seen. When she
began to sing folk music in costume, I left. There was
something indecent and barbarously cruel about this
business.'[18]

'At the intermission,' Davis's review continued, 'Mme.
Jenkins was all but swamped by a procession of ushers,

each bearing a huge basket of flowers. The stage crew piled them on, and grouped them around the piano, and for the second half of the programme the elderly thrush might have been in a greenhouse chirping through an open pane.'[19] More than a hundred individual floral offerings had been sent to the Hall for her.

'In the early 80s I was able to talk to people who were at the Carnegie Hall concert and none of them remembered the same event,' says playwright Steven Temperley.

Florence herself was ecstatic. Greeting guests in her dressing room after her performance, she turned to Mera Weinstock, who had overseen her Melotone recording sessions and, blushing, asked: 'Don't you think I had real courage to sing the *Queen of the Night* again after that wonderful recording I made of it at the studio?' Weinstock, who was also the director of the New York-based promoters the Concert Artists' Guild, was apparently speechless. As Milton Bendiner recalled, 'Madame Jenkins believed that she would never again attain the heights she had reached in her recorded singing of the aria. Truthfully, those who had heard the recording heartily concurred in this opinion.'[20] Quick to react, the comedian George Bernard (who would star in the 1952 film *Gobs and Gals*) added an impression of Florence to his stage act.

In an entry in his diary, St. Clair summed up the night in four short words: 'recital a great success'.

10 Goodbye

Mocked by one unnamed critic as 'a bizarre demon-stration of her vocal inability',[1] Madame's greatest accomplishment would also prove to be her last perfor-mance. Florence suffered a heart attack five days after the concert while visiting G. Schirmer's Music Store on East 43rd Street, and was confined to her bed. St. Clair insisted that she had help, and a Nurse Haggard was taken on to attend to her. However she passed away just a short month after her triumph, at her rooms in the Hotel Seymour in Manhattan, at around 7:30 pm on Sunday, 26 November 1944.

Her death came as a shock to St. Clair: although she had been sleepy in the afternoon, that morning she had appeared bright and alert, and he had no qualms about leaving her to dine at the Gotham Hotel (on Fifth Avenue, now the Peninsula) with their mutual friend (and Florence's rumoured lover), the Russian émigré Prince Galitzin that evening. On hearing that she had taken a turn for the worse he rushed to be at her side. When he arrived at her suite Florence's friend Dorothy informed him that he had arrived too late. That night he wrote in his diary 'After 36 years of happiness in love, B.

MRS. FLORENCE F. JENKINS

Founder of Verdi Club Gave Recital Here on Oct. 25

Mrs. Florence Foster Jenkins, soprano, founder and president of the Verdi Club, died last night at her residence, the Hotel Seymour, 50 West Forty-fifth Street, after an illness of three weeks. She was the widow of Dr. Frank Jenkins of Washington, D. C.

Mrs. Jenkins, who had also been president of the New York League of American Penwomen, gave a recital in Carnegie Hall on Oct. 25, in which she was assisted by the Pascarella Chamber Music Society Quartet, Cosme McMoon, pianist, and Oeste De Sevo, flutist.

No immediate relatives survive.

Florence's obituary in the *New York Times,* 27 November 1944.

leaves me ... The sky shed tears.' She was seventy-seven.

Some would claim that her death was the result of a broken heart caused by the more scathing reviews of her final show. 'I opposed the concert at Carnegie Hall,' St. Clair told Florence Stevenson of *Opera News* a decade after her death. 'I didn't think a person of her age should take on that strain. It sucks you dry. My wife would be alive today if she'd stuck to her regular Ritz concert. I didn't want her to sing after her voice was worn out, but she was adamant. "I can do it," she told me. "I'll show everybody." Her friends loved her so; they couldn't criticise her voice. Well, it turned out the fiasco I expected. Afterwards, when we went home, Florence was upset – and when she read the reviews, crushed. She had not known, you see.'[2] She was, as Richard Connema recalled, visibly shaken by the ruckus that accompanied her Carnegie Hall performance, but she could not have been completely ignorant of her critics. Florence and St. Clair dutifully filed away every mention of her they came across in a scrapbook that was later donated, along with St. Clair's diaries and other papers, to the Billy Rose Theatre Collection of the New York Public Library. The clippings include some of her less savoury notices: Florence must have known that some of these commentators were ridiculing her. Clearly she was more aware of criticism than St. Clair gave her credit for, for when Hearst's *American Weekly* chose to poke fun in an article titled 'The Society Songbird who Sprouts Wings Once a Year' – calling her 'the only known diva to achieve fame via the Bronx cheer and come back for more'[3] – she felt forced to defend herself. Contacted by the New York-born but Sydney-based journalist Lindsay Clinch for his syndicated column 'New York Round Up', she told him 'I'm much too busy for interviews, but there is one thing about that article I do not like. It says I give one concert a year. That's not true: I give several.'[4]

Time magazine afforded her passing just two lines: 'Died: Florence Foster Jenkins, 76, billowing coloratura, well-to-do sponsor of her own costumed concerts at Manhattan's Ritz-Carlton Hotel; one month after her Carnegie Hall recital debut (where her rose-petal-strewn rendition of Clavelitos was wildly bravoed); of a heart attack; in Manhattan.'[5]

Services were held in New York the following Tuesday, where 'the chapel was filled with friends of the deceased. A harpist gave two selections; a baritone sang "Going Home" and "The Lord's Prayer"'[6] before her body was returned to Wilkes-Barre. In his diary St. Clair wrote that he 'felt some comfort after I had kissed her and held her little hand. The heavens wept.' She was buried in the Foster family mausoleum on 30 November. St. Clair was not present, and the local paper (the *Wilkes-Barre Record*) could not be bothered to check his name: 'H Clair Hayfield, who handled Mrs. Jenkins's musical affairs, was unable to come here for today's service.'[7] For several years after his beloved Bunny's death, on the anniversary of her birthday, St. Clair sent flowers to the Foster mausoleum in Wilkes-Barre, and he had a seat dedicated with her name at the theatre in Abingdon, Virginia. A few weeks following the funeral, going through boxes of her belongings at their West 37th Street apartment, St. Clair found the letters he had written to her when they first met, all tied together with a blue ribbon: 'very poor letters I thought [but] how she must have loved me to take such care of them', he noted in his diary.

'In her own way,' wrote Winfield Sargeant in *Life* magazine a few months after her death, 'She had achieved the goal of every hopeful artist who walks on to the stage. She died famous.' Writing about her Carnegie Hall concert Robert Bagar, of the *New York World-Telegram*, filed what became a fitting epitaph: 'She was exceedingly happy in her work. It is a pity so few artists are. And the happiness was communicated as if by magic to her hearers, who were stimulated to the point of audible cheering, even joyous laughter and ecstasy by the inimitable singing.'[8]

In January 1945 members of the Verdi Club held a special memorial in her honour, with St. Clair giving a talk on his beloved Bunny: 'the last meeting of the old Verdi Club,' he noted in his diary, 'of which darling B. presided from November 28 '17 until her death. I was sad and emotional.' That same month a spiteful piece of prose by Irving Johnson appeared in the *American Weekly* magazine. Labelling her 'the tone-dumb darling of the tone-deaf', Johnson's article stated that 'in Florence Foster Jenkins' bright lexicon of age a ripe tomato was an orchid and the faintest hiss a roar of applause. Bronx cheers were her bread and butter, over-aged eggs the food of her fame. The world was her eggplant – so long as thousands came to jeer and toss.'[9] At least Johnson was pleasant about Cosme, whom he called 'patient' and 'heroic'.

Cosme himself later revealed that, as far as he was aware, Madame had intended her fortune to be put to use after her death to establish a trust to pay for scholarships for talented singers, to be known as the Florence Foster Jenkins Memorial. Sadly she died intestate. Kathleen Bayfield insisted that Florence always carried her will and other important documents with her in an attaché case (described by St. Clair as a 'valise, canvas and brown leather [with] two brass locks') which – just as had happened when her own father passed away thirty-five years earlier – mysteriously went missing. McMoon was adamant that she had not in fact written a will 'owing to the lady's superstition that a will was an invitation to death'. Johnson's article claimed that she 'left a pile of bank notes in banks she had forgotten all about. She also left a fortune in cash, real estate and jewelry'.[10] In a recording made in 1970 by the pianist Bruce Hungerford,[11] Kathleen Bayfield and several of Florence's other acquaintances claimed that McMoon was involved, along with her maid Mildred Brown, in the theft of her will. Finding that Florence had left no money to either of them, they are said to have burned it. In February 1946 Cosme and Mildred attempted to sue the estate for $25,000; in that same recording Adolf Pollitz claimed that he was asked to testify in court against McMoon (he *was* enlisted by St. Clair to help back up his own claim). 'Yes, Cosme McMoon put in a claim but it was dismissed by the Surrogate Court,' Nancy Schimmel said. 'He had 30 days in which to appeal. He did not pursue it, and her estate went to the Bulford and Hoagland heirs.'

St. Clair continued to act sporadically after Florence died, although his mannered, old-fashioned style had fallen out of fashion. Without Florence's money to support him he was virtually destitute, and he spent months locked in a bitter clash with her heirs for a share of her estate. His friends rallied around him but, as he notes in his diaries, his eyes were often 'filled with tears thinking of B'.

'He wept greatly,' Kay later said. 'All the glamour of the past 36 years was over. No more parties, no more Verdi Club, the cycle had been broken. He could hardly bear to walk the streets where they had been together.' On the stroke of midnight on 31 December, as 1944 became 1945, St. Clair 'placed an empty chair opposite me and drank to her, imagining her rising opposite me as she has done on this anniversary for countless years'. Several times after her death, still mourning her loss, St. Clair experienced what he considered to be supernatural experiences, and one of these incidents rattled him enough to mention it in a letter to Kay that summer:

> I have never had any truck with spiritualism or clairvoyance, (and) when I awoke in the middle of the night and heard a knocking, I disregarded it and told myself I must not be fooled. But when some nights later I awoke for no reason, and then heard a secret knock, very distinctly, in the north room of 66 (their apartment). I went in the dark and talked to Florence but gained no response. Thinking this was a wish I

should communicate, I went to a spiritualist. Aware
that these people usually preyed on thought reading,
I was astonished when certain things were mentioned
which I myself did not know until afterwards verified. Also the message said: 'I am very unhappy you
should be suffering because of lack of care on my part.
There was a will but it has been destroyed. I love you
and shall always love you as much as I ever did with
my whole heart, and I send you my blessings. In three
months your financial position will be improved, so do
not worry. Attend to your stage work to avoid it. Trust
in God more than you ever did before, above all I want
you to be happy. Bless you, bless you, bless you.' The
other things mentioned were about her father, and not
until I verified them did I know them, so that could
not have been thought reading.

According to St. Clair's diary (February 1945) the
spiritualist Beulah Brown 'made astoundingly correct
statements about B. I suffered very badly from emotional upset.' He would consult with Ms. Brown on several occasions, and began to attend a Spiritualist Church
in the vain hope of hearing from his beloved Bunny. On
Hallowe'en 1945, and again on 14 January 1946 – the
anniversary of their first meeting – he claimed to have
received messages from her spirit.

Unfairly described in court as a retired Shakespearian
actor and opera baritone (he had hardly retired: he was
back on stage, in the play *Hand in Glove*, a little less

than a week after Florence died, followed that with an appearance in the play *Merely Coincidental* and in December took part in a screen test for MGM), St. Clair wanted more than just the right to administer her estate: he wanted the world to know that he and Florence had, in fact, been common-law husband and wife. After a protracted legal battle her eroded but still substantial bank balance – Florence's personal worth was something in the region of $100,000, equivalent to more than $1.3 million today (2016) – was awarded to her relatives. Florence's cousin, Mrs. Ella Bulford Harvey, was appointed administrator of both Florence's worldly goods and the remains of Charles Foster's estate in July 1945, with fourteen cousins and at least four other relatives all vying for a piece of the pie. St. Clair, with the help of Nurse Haggard, Edythe Totten (a friend of Florence's who was also the president of the National Round Table Club and the Drama Club), Adolf Pollitz and others, issued a claim against the estate for $20,000, money his first attorney Louis Halle insisted he was due for the amount of work he put in on behalf of the Verdi Club over the course of more than a quarter of a century; Halle also persuaded St. Clair to join with Cosme in a legal application requesting a search for Florence's missing will.

Although his common-law husband suit was never established, the cousins settled with St. Clair out of court, with him receiving a cheque for $22,000 on 30

August 1945. While the court case continued, he kept up his correspondence with Kay Weatherly, now living in Dorset, England, writing to tell her about how lost and alone he felt. In one he wrote:

My life entirely circled round hers whilst Florence lived, if I were in necessity, she would provide for me, and if she died first I was to inherit her personal estate. My statements of her promises are corroborated by three witnesses to whom she said much the same thing, but even if this claim were successful it would produce nothing for twelve months, and then much less than my claim. A mere pittance, yet she intended me to inherit all her estate, of that I am perfectly sure.

Many of their mutual friends agreed that this had indeed been Florence's intention, yet few were willing to stand up in court and attest to the fact.

According to Nancy Schimmel, Florence's cousin, 'Her belongings were sold at an auction and any money she had was divided among her living heirs. Royalties from her recordings were also received by the heirs.' The auction took place on 26 June 1945: St. Clair attended, but wrote that it was 'too heartbreaking, so I did not remain long. Bought the dear little table at which I had sat so often.' He managed to keep a few items, reminders of his life with Florence, including some of the pictures which hung on the walls of her suite at the Hotel Seymour, and a bracelet which – when he had it appraised in March

1946 – was valued at $6,000. He had been given a verbal promise by the attorney acting for the estate, Polzer, that he would receive the rights to her records. The two-storey brick house at 27 South Franklin Street, where Florence had spent her childhood, was torn down to make way for a parking lot in 1946.

Kay Weatherly returned to New York on 20 January 1946, and on 27 January, fourteen years after they first met and two days before her birthday, the pair were married at St. Stephen's Episcopal Church, West 69th Street, New York. After dinner St. Clair returned to his small apartment, reduced to half the size it once was since the beginning of May to save on rent (he was now paying $43.50 a month for the one room, plus the use of a kitchen and bathroom on the floor above); Kay stayed at the Iroquois Hotel. Shortly after investing his money in an annuity they bought an unimposing house at 24 Wildwood Road, Larchmont, New York, later moving to a smaller house in nearby Elm Avenue where they lived for the rest of St. Clair's life. His relationship with Kay was just as unconventional as the one he had enjoyed with Florence: St. Clair's much younger wife had a voracious appetite for sex and, after an accident made her ageing husband virtually impotent, she was involved a string of affairs with much younger men.

Finale

A decade after her death, eight of Florence's recordings were gathered together by RCA on the 10-inch album *A Florence! Foster!! Jenkins!!! Recital!!!!* Compiled from her Melotone recordings by George Marek, who had become Artists and Repertoire manager at RCA, it was described by him as 'the worst record of the year ... no, make that 10 years!' Her first nationally available release, *A Florence! Foster!! Jenkins!!! Recital!!!!* kick-started the cult of Florence, with a number of writers weighing in with their thoughts and reminiscences. 'To this day, no one can say for certain whether Mme. Jenkins was as naively – shall we say lousy? – an artist as she seemed, or whether she was pulling everyone's leg. The odds are that she was serious about her Art,' wrote the critic Mel Heimer in his nationally syndicated column 'My New York' in April 1954. 'It would seem that the old girl climbed to fame with a kind of sincere wretchedness.' One of the kinder reviews of the release, which appeared in the *Buffalo Courier-Express,* stated that 'her "singing" sounds like that of the amateur recitalist, with the same off-key notes that make such programs often amusing. However. Mme. Jenkins gets close enough in such difficult arias as "The Bell Song" from "Lakme" to indicate that she could have made it with another half tone of range.' Irving Kolodin wrote that 'she rarely sang on pitch, and she rarely ended a song or an aria with the note the composer intended. But she persisted from first to last with a complete seriousness that had her devotees literally rolling in the aisles.'[1]

Gregor Benko feels that the myth of Florence as a dotty dowager began with the release of *A Florence! Foster!! Jenkins!!! Recital!!!!* and its accompanying sleeve note:

> The fiction that Jenkins was a batty but loveable old lady was created by Francis Robinson, an assistant manager at the Metropolitan Opera House at the time RCA Victor issued the first LP issue of her recordings. Bending the truth that way is understandable – it was a different world, for one thing, and not many would have wanted to read a liner note about how awful Jenkins was as a person. Robinson certainly personally knew what monstrously vain creatures many opera stars under his purview were in real life, but he was a master at spinning inspirational and colorful tales about singers. So he created this myth of Jenkins, which has proved enduring and irresistible.

'The difference between Madame Jenkins and other artists is simple. Other artists occasionally hit a wrong note. Madame Jenkins occasionally hit a right note,' said

George Marek. In an interview to publicise the release of *A Florence! Foster!! Jenkins!!! Recital!!!!* he recalled attending one of her Ritz-Carlton performances: 'It was her custom to give one concert a year. The price was $5, and in many ways it was worth it.' The same tracks were later made available on the 1962 collection *The Glory (????) of the Human Voice*, padded out with *A Faust Travesty* by Jenny Williams and Thomas Burns. In the August 1962 edition of *High Fidelity* magazine, Conrad Osborne described this as 'an aural sick joke' and went on to say that 'these records do not seem funny at all, but pathetic, and even annoying. I cannot imagine any-one's playing them more than three or four times, except by way of De Sade-esque experiment.' How wrong he was: *Life* magazine called it 'the funniest LP in years'.[2] More recent CD compilations have pulled all nine of Florence's extant performances together. Sadly no other recordings, nor any film footage, have ever surfaced.

St. Clair Bayfield's acting career was all but over by the end of the 1940s. His last appearance on Broadway was as Henry Wheeler (described as 'a wacky grand-father') in the 1948 production of the two-act com-edy *For Heaven's Sake, Mother!*; that same year he also returned to London, appearing at the Lyric Theatre, Hammersmith in George Bernard Shaw's *Captain Brassbound's Conversion* with Dame Flora Robson. However, he kept himself busy into old age. Much to Kay's annoyance, he continued to wear the wedding

The sleeve of the French release of *The Glory (???) of the Human Voice* featured an exclusive design by noted illustrator Jean-Claude Trambouze.

ring that Florence had given him – but on his fourth finger. She eventually managed to persuade him to take it off after she had a ring made for him featuring his family crest. He continued to write, in 1951 registering the copyright for a self-penned three-act play called *Count Fosco*, which he based on the novel *The Woman in White* by Wilkie Collins, and passed away quietly at home on 20 May 1967 at the age of ninety-one. His obituary in the *New York Times* made no mention of Florence.

The following April, a plaque in his honour was unveiled at the Larchmont Public Library, which both he and Florence had helped set up back in 1922 – he as producer and actor, she as patron – with a fundraising performance of *A Midsummer Night's Dream*. His widow Kay helped establish an annual prize for Shakespearian actors in his name: the St. Clair Bayfield Award, administered by the Actors' Equity Association, is given to the best actor or actress in a non-featured role in a Shakespearian production.

At the time of his death, St. Clair had been working on the manuscript of a book about Florence, tentatively titled *Hearts and Clubs*, an idea first suggested to him by his friend, the author Gilbert Maxwell, in June 1945; Kay took over this work but altered the text so much, ridiculing Florence and boosting her own importance in her story, that it was refused by the only publisher who ever saw it. His papers, including his diaries, were donated to the Billy Rose Theatre Collection of the New York Public Library. Sadly, the manuscript of the book was not included. All that remains is the section which Kay herself narrates on the Hungerford Tape: a highly flawed and somewhat mean-spirited account of Florence's life with St. Clair. 'She stole 36 years of the best years of St. Clair's life,' she told friends, 'fourteen of which I waited for him.'

It is thought that, after St. Clair died, Kay Bayfield destroyed what was left of the six hundred or so love letters that Florence had sent to him. She despised Florence for not letting him go to her, and often maligned her. St. Clair had offered these letters to his attorneys as evidence of their relationship, but had burned many of them himself in October and November 1945 – presumably at Kay's request – around the first anniversary of Florence's death. It's perfectly possible that any film footage that once existed has also been destroyed.

Cosme McMoon would continue to teach piano and write music. The sister of the sculptor Patricia Volk was one of his many students, and she states that he used to 'rap her fingers with a pencil when she hit a wrong note'.[3] The year after Florence passed away he composed the music for the ballet scene in the Broadway musical *The Would-be Gentleman*, adapted from the Molière play *Le Bourgeois Gentilhomme* by former vaudeville comedian Bobby Clark. When money became tight he supplemented his income by looking after the accounts for a gay bathhouse and judging bodybuilding contests. There is a famous photograph from 1974 of Cosme being lifted up by Arnold Schwarzenegger and Bob Birdsong at that year's Mr. Olympia competition, at the Felt Forum in Madison Square Gardens. Schwarzenegger won his fifth consecutive Mr. Olympia title that year.

Since McMoon's death several people have come forward to claim that he wound up running a gay escort service attached to the Mid Town Gym on New York's 42nd Street. 'I happened to know three individuals who knew McMoon and his circumstances in his later life,' says Gregor Benko. 'One of these actually had a few piano lessons with McMoon as an adolescent. He subsequently had recourse to encounter McMoon when he was managing the male brothel associated with the gym in Manhattan's then seedy Times Square area. He was a customer of the brothel, McMoon the manager.' Other people who knew him have strenuously denied this. According to his nephew Mark McMunn:

> We think these stories were perhaps started by some people that were envious of Florence Foster Jenkins' notoriety and began spreading rumors about everyone that was associated with her. Cosme was not a spiteful person and knowing him he would have would have told us to ignore these stories.
>
> For the remainder of his life he continued to perform, teach, and write music. After the mid-1950s he would annually drive across country from New York to California to visit his youngest brother Jim, and his wife in California, but would first stop in San Antonio to visit his mother, brother and nephew [Mark] in San Antonio. Every year when he would stay with us he would always tell my father that when his time came he wanted him to bring him home to San Antonio. His remains are in the same cemetery as two of his brothers.
>
> He lived very quietly and modestly, and was very independent even to his last days. He became ill with pancreatic cancer in the summer of 1980. A neighbor

contacted his family in San Antonio [to tell them] that Cosme was ill. Cosme's nephew William went to New York to arrange to bring him to San Antonio. Jim McMunn, Cosme's youngest sibling, flew into New York from Los Angeles to assist. Cosme was brought back to San Antonio in August 1980, and lived for two more days before passing away. As Cosme requested his remains were cremated, and his ashes are resting at Sunset Memorial Park in San Antonio.

I think he would like to be remembered as a great instructor. Being one of his students I can tell you first hand that he had the ability to explain a composition in a way that any ordinary person could understand it. It is my hope that the public will come to the realisation that it took a pianist of extraordinary ability to be Florence Foster Jenkins' accompanist.

'I believe that Florence thought very highly of Cosme McMoon or she would not have retained him as her pianist,' adds Nancy Schimmel. 'The critics have not been kind to him nor to Florence so I can sympathise with his family. With each new story that appears, it becomes more ludicrous. Florence's family do not think of Cosme as a scoundrel but as a very talented pianist.' Adolf Pollitz, no fan himself of McMoon (he called him 'a rotter' on the Hungerford Tape and insisted that Madame had intended to fire him) once stated that Cosme never said anything derogatory about Florence, and that St. Clair was never rude about Cosme either.

St. Clair himself was certain that Cosme had not taken Florence's will, even though Pollitz was convinced that McMoon had 'made away with her other bag'.

Florence's extraordinary life has provided the inspiration for imitators, cartoons, puppets and several plays. Sid and Marty Krofft's 1961 show *Les Poupees de Paris* featured a twittering diva called Mrs. Jenkins Foster, and it has been suggested by several Hergé aficionados (including the French writer Bruno Costemalle in his 2007 book *But Where is the Head of Mozart?*[4]) that Bianca Castafiore, the narcissistic, whimsical and absent-minded diva who appears in several Tintin adventures was based, at least in part, on Florence. *Precious Few*, written by Terry Sneed, which had its debut performance in Little Rock, Arkansas in 1994, was the first of many stage shows and plays to draw from Florence's life, and his account of Florence and Cosme's relationship won the 1997 Ingram Fellowship in Playwriting. In 1999 she was portrayed in *Goddess of Song* by South African playwright Charles J. Fourie, and 2001 saw Florence the subject of Chris Balance's play *Viva la Diva*. In 2004 Judith Paris brought her to life in her one-woman, one-act play *When Florence met Isadora*, and she was portrayed by British stage and screen star Maureen Lipman in Peter Quilter's musical *Glorious!* in 2005, the same year that *Souvenir*, by Broadway playwright Stephen Temperley debuted, with the Tony Award-winning actress Judy Kaye as Florence. 'Florence would have been pleased to know that we broke all box office records, ever, when we performed in Birmingham,' Lipman told the *Guardian's* Lisa Allardice. '*Glorious!* is delightful, it's batty, it's absurd and it involves the audience almost as if they were at a pantomime. I'm kind of honoured to be in her somewhat shaky spotlight. Her story is one of triumph over embarrassment. If you have the will and the stamina and the self-belief, you will triumph, even if, like Florence, you've been dead for 60 years when you finally get your true recognition.'[5]

Stephen Temperley has his own opinion of Florence's art: 'In New York in the late 60s Mrs. Jenkins would be referred to in an off-hand way. A friend brought the record (*The Glory??? of the Human Voice*) to a Sunday brunch. We played it and everyone laughed. After a few minutes I stopped laughing because I don't really think it's funny. In my opinion the real woman was something else. It's not that she couldn't sing: if one listens to her recordings one can hear that she has no voice, which is a different thing.'

Souvenir, subtitled *A Fantasia on the Life of Florence Foster Jenkins*, has been a worldwide success but, as the author explains, although audiences love his version of Florence, Temperley's play was never meant to be a tribute.

My play really has very little to do with the real woman, although I did research her background and life, which is why it's subtitled 'a fantasia'. I used the fact that she couldn't sing and invented her devotion to art and to music. My Cosme is a complete invention; he never accompanied himself in a piano bar, as he does in my play. I cut myself completely free of the details of what 'actually' happened, partly because the whole thing is shrouded in gossip and the kind of spiteful innuendo so beloved by a certain segment of our world. As my Florence says at one point 'The sort [of people] who go to first nights at the opera in order to laugh.'

People who see the play imagine that my Florence, with her total, blind belief in herself represents the real woman – she doesn't. To this day, people in New York believe that Cosme was in fact the famous accompanist Edwin McArthur. In my play the man is at the centre, it is his story as he tries to cope with the increasingly insane demands of what would appear to be a mad-woman. But the audience does love Flo!

Like Temperley, Peter Quilter first became aware of the magic of Florence Foster Jenkins through a friend, who gave him a cassette featuring her recording of the *Queen of the Night* aria.

I was intrigued and went to the English National Opera bookshop to ask if they had a CD or anything. When I asked about Florence, both guys behind the counter instantly smiled. At that very second I knew there was a potential play brewing. She pursued her dream in spite of everybody trying to get in her way.

She ignored the laughter, maintained her determination, and charged forward. Initially I set out to write a comedy about a terrible singer, but it became a play about pursuing your goals and fulfilling your dreams and desires regardless of whether you're any good at it.

Glorious! was an instant success. Peter Quilter goes on:

Within a year of writing it, the play was on stage in London's West End, Olivier award-nominated for Best New Comedy and within five years it had played in 25 countries. It offers a great role for a funny actress and people are fascinated by the story. It took off immediately and still receives dozens of productions every year. My purpose was not to write any kind of documentary. It is not the job of theatre plays (especially comedies) to be accurate. The job was to take the essence of a story and make it compelling, amusing, dramatic. I think it does capture the spirit of the people but with the characters adjusted in order to fully exploit the humour of the situation and the potential for relationships and emotions. So Cosme has been given a very dry sense of humour and St. Clair has been made more extrovert. He's not as good an actor in my play as he was in real life, for example, because it helped the audience understand the relationship of St. Clair and Florence and it granted more opportunities for comedy. As a writer my first question is not 'is this 100% accurate?' but 'is this 100% funny?'

In 2007 singer-turned documentary filmmaker Donald Collup collaborated with the writer and researcher Gregor Benko on *A World of Her Own*, the first serious attempt at a filmed documentary of Florence's life. Says Collup:

> I met Gregor Benko around 2004. He told me of the research he had been doing for the previous twenty years on Jenkins. I had just finished my first documentary [*Never Before: The Life, Art and First New York Career of Astrid Varnay*] and said to myself: this screams documentary! He and I started working on it days later. I was attracted to the project not only because of the colorful and rich stories surrounding her, but the fact the public was unaware that this woman was suffering from a disease that dare not say its name. And then the devastating day after Carnegie Hall, she finds out her entire career has been a joke to the public. I find this so tragic.

Florence's career provided the inspiration for the 2015 French/Czech co-production *Marguerite*, with Catherine Frot portraying Marguerite Dumont, a socialite and aspiring opera singer (named after the redoubtable Margaret Dumont, the actress best remembered as the comic foil to the Marx Brothers) who believes she has a beautiful voice, and now the world will see Florence light up the silver screen in Stephen Frears' new film, when Meryl Streep takes on her mantle. The doting

St. Clair Bayfield is played by Hugh Grant, with Simon Helberg – best known for playing Howard in the hit TV comedy *The Big Bang Theory* – as the long-suffering Cosme McMoon.

'The thing about her was the great joy she took in doing it and how much she loved music and that she was conveying that as well,' Streep told *Empire* magazine. 'She underwrote Toscanini's Carnegie Hall seasons every year. She generously gave ... Nobody would line up for bad singing: it's the other thing, the human yearning to meet music wherever music lives. Hilarity ensues, but there's also joy. There's something else as to why people wanted to see her.'[6]

The release of *Florence Foster Jenkins* is just one of the events that will help keep Madame's name in the spotlight in 2016: German director Ralf Pleger is making a ninety-minute drama-documentary about Florence, *The Florence Foster Jenkins Story*, featuring American opera star Joyce DiDonato. Perhaps unsurprisingly, Pleger was also introduced to Florence via *The Glory (???) of the Human Voice*: 'I had my earphones on, and then the music came, and it put a smile on my face' he told the *Wilkes-Barre Citizen's Voice* on the first day of shooting. 'It was a beautiful experience, because no matter how bad she sang, she sang with not a single sign of insecurity, and I think that's the impressive part.' Bringing her unique presence right into the twenty-first century, there are even a game and smartphone app planned.

The late David Bowie was a fan; Barbra Streisand is too. Bowie discussed her at length in an Australian TV interview and later wrote about his introduction to Florence in a 2013 *Vanity Fair* article:

> In the mid- to late 70s, Norman Fisher, art and people collector, threw the most diverse soirées in the whole of New York. People from every sector of the so and not so avant-garde would flock to his tiny down-town apartment just because Norman was a magnet. Charismatic, huge fun, and brilliant at introducing all the right people to the wrong people. His musical taste was as frothy as he himself. Two of his recommenda-tions have stayed with me over the years. One was *Manhattan Tower*, the first radio musical by Gordon Jenkins [no relation to Florence], and the other *The Glory (????) of the Human Voice*.[7]

In 1976 Streisand was compared to Madame by reviewer Joseph McLellan: 'not perhaps since the immortal Florence Foster Jenkins had the kind of opportunity pre-sented by a new Columbia record album titled *Classical Barbra*. Streisand sings better than Jenkins (almost any-one does), but she offers essentially the same opportunity: to hear a really bad performance of classical music.'[8]

'Many have tried to imitate her, but without success,' her ever-loyal accompanist Cosme McMoon stated. 'The reason is that they were not as sincere in their efforts as Madame Jenkins was. She is inimitable.'

'Florence Jenkins was kind and generous,' wrote Mozelle Bennett Sawyer, 'A fine person. It was her obvious sincerity that made people laugh. Of course she heard the laughter, but she only thought she was bringing happiness to her audiences, and she laughed with them.'[9]

St. Clair Bayfield, still grieving over the loss of his beloved Bunny, summed up the magic of Florence – and explained her enduring appeal – better than anyone else could:

> Why did she go on singing? Singing was her only form of self-expression. She had perfect rhythm. Her interpretation was good and her languages wonderful. She had star quality. There was something about her singing that made everyone look at her. People may have laughed at her singing, but the applause was real. She was a natural born musician. But instrument – there was very little instrument. I think my wife knew her voice was passing, but she loved singing so much she determined to continue with it.
>
> She only ever thought of making other people happy. That is why it is so unkind, so unfair, all this ridicule of her.[10]

A Florence! Foster!! Jenkins!!! Timeline!!!!

♪ 1836 November 25 – Charles Dorrance Foster, Florence's father, is born in Dallas Township, Luzerne County. PA.

♪ 1851 February – Mary Jane Hoagland, Florence's mother, is born in Flemington, New Jersey.

♪ 1852 Date unknown – Francis 'Frank' Thornton Jenkins is born in Baltimore.

♪ 1868 July 19 – Narcissa Florence Foster is born to Charles and Mary Foster in Wilkes-Barre, Pennsylvania.

♪ 1875 Date unknown – Lillian Blanche 'Lilly' Foster is born in Wilkes-Barre.
August 2 – St. Clair Bayfield is born in Cheltenham, England.

♪ 1876 Date unknown – FF plays her first concert as a pianist in Philadelphia (*Wilkes-Barre Times-Leader*, 2004).

♪ 1878 July 3 – FF sings (and possibly plays piano) during a visit to Wilkes-Barre by President Hayes.

♪ 1880 June 15 – Frank Thornton Jenkins receives his medical doctorate (*Philadelphia Enquirer*, 16 March 1881).

♪ 1881 July 25 – FF is a featured pianist at the Säengerfest, held at the City Hall Gardens, Wilkes-Barre (*Wilkes-Barre Record,* 26 July 1881).

♪ 1883 June – FF graduates from Mrs. Kutz's Seminary for Young Ladies, on West Walnut St, Philadelphia, taking a gold medal for elocution (*Wilkes-Barre Record*, 23 June 1883).
June 29 – Lillian Blanche 'Lilly' Foster dies
July 1 – Lilly Foster is buried in Huntsville (*Wilkes-Barre Record*, 2 July 1883).

♪ 1884 Date unknown (before September) – FF 'elopes' to Philadelphia with Dr. Frank Thornton Jenkins.

♪ 1885 February 14 – FFJ is reported to be staying at Laurel-in-the-Pines, a luxurious hotel in Lakewood, New Jersey (*The Times*, Philadelphia).

♪ 1886 August 20 – FFJ (as Mrs. Dr. Jenkins) and her parents are reported as staying at the United States Hotel, Saratoga Springs (*Daily Saratogan,* 20 August 1886).

♪ 1887 June 26 – Florence is mentioned in the society column of a local newspaper as staying at the Wetherill (hotel): 'Mrs. Jenkins is one of Philadelphia's most noted performers on the piano' (*The Times*, Philadelphia 26 June 1887).

♪ 1888 May – FFJ graduates head of the class at the
       Philadelphia Conservatory of Music.

♪ 1895 Date unknown – Florence, as Mrs. Frank T. Jenkins,
       is listed as a graduate of the Philadelphia Musical
       Academy in the Academy's Silver Jubilee programme.

♪ 1898 October – Frank Jenkins is now operating from an
       office in the Gluck Building, Niagara Falls, adver-
       tising as a 'Specialist in Treatment of Diseases of
       Throat, Nose, Ear and Lungs' (*Niagara Falls Gazette*,
       various issues, October 1898 to March 1899).

♪ 1901 February 22 – Cosme McMunn (later Anglicised to
       McMoon) is born in Durango, Mexico.

♪ 1902 August – FFJ sues Frank for divorce (*Buffalo Evening
       News*, 8 August 1902).

♪ 1903 January 10 – 'One of the prettiest girls seen here
       this season is Miss Florence Foster Jenkins of
       Philadelphia. She and Mrs. Charles Balderston are
       spending several weeks in the Laurel-in-the-Pines.'
       (*New York Press*, 11 January 1903).
       February 25 – FFJ, in Washington with the
       Pennsylvania delegation of the Daughters of the
       American Revolution, is a guest at a reception in the
       home of Mrs. Randolph Keim (*Philadelphia Inquirer,*
       26 February 1903).

♪ 1905 March – Dr. Frank Thornton Jenkins is now resident
       in Washington, D.C.

♪ 1906 December 31 – FFJ plays piano (accompanying a recitation by Mrs. Vaughan) at a meeting of the Euterpe Club (*New York Herald,* 6 January 1907).

♪ 1907 April 13 – The *New York Times* reported that FFJ and one G. Wallach had a judgment lodged in court against them and were ordered to pay $241 as debtors – the article mentions that FFJ was 'not summoned', so did not appear in court (*New York Times*, 14 April 1907).
September 24 – Edwin McArthur is born in Denver, Colorado.

♪ 1909 January 14 – St. Clair Bayfield and FFJ meet for the first time at the Waldorf-Astoria, at a meeting of the Euterpe Club, where she was chairman of music.
August – St. Clair arrives back in New York after his trip to England to break off his engagement.
August 16 – FFJ and St. Clair take part in a 'marriage' ceremony in front of friends at the Hotel Vanderbilt (*PM Daily,* 1945).
September 29 – Charles Dorrance Foster dies in Wilkes-Barre after several months' illness.
October 1 – The funeral of C.D. Foster is held at St. Stephen's Church, Wilkes-Barre, followed by an internment at the Foster mausoleum at Hollenback Cemetery.
October – FFJ and Mary Hoagland Foster appear in court as witnesses in the case of Charles Foster's missing will.

♪ **1910** Date unknown – Mary and Florence move permanently to New York.

October – Charles Foster's estate is finally settled, in Mary and FFJ's favour.

December 14 – 'After months of rehearsing by the young women members of the choral of the New York Mozart Society, the first concert and dance of the second season's series will be held in the grand ballroom of the Hotel Astor'. FFJ is listed as one of the members of the choral group (*New York Herald*, 11 December 1910).

♪ **1911** Date unknown – The McMunn family is forced to leave Mexico, settling in San Antonio, Texas.

December 20 – The New York Mozart Society opens its third season of evening concerts at the Hotel Astor. FFJ is listed as a member of the society's choral group (*New York Herald*, 24 December 1911).

♪ **1912** January 5 – The New Yorkers hold their second musical and literary social meeting of the season at the Hotel Astor under the direction of FFJ. 'There will be a dramatic sketch by Miss Pauline P. Aldrich, in which the characters will be played by Mrs. Florence Foster Jenkins and Mr. Henry Gaines Hawn' (*New York Herald*, 31 December 1911).

March 24 – 'Mrs. Florence Foster Jenkins, who was the chairman of the entertainment and musicale given at the Plaza recently for the Euterpe Club's philanthropic fund, reports that a gratifying amount of money was realized' (*New York Herald*, 24 March 1912).

April 12 – FFJ hosts 'an informal dance for the young persons who took part in the entertainments for the Euterpe Club's philanthropic fund at the Plaza recently' at the Waldorf-Astoria (*New York Herald*, 7 April 1912).

May 10 – The Twilight Club hosts some of New York's criminal underclass at a 'rather unusual dinner at the Aldine Club. The subject of discussion will be the 'Relation of the Thief to Society'. FFJ is one of the organising committee (*New York Times*, 5 May 1912). November 21 – FFJ is honoured at a musical morning and luncheon at the Waldorf-Astoria, held by the Euterpe Club (*New York Press*, 24 November 1912). November 29/30 – FFJ helps look after the cake table at the annual bazaar and musical festival of the Knickerbocker Relief Club, held at the Waldorf-Astoria (*The Sun* (New York), 1 December 1912).

♪ 1913 March 24 – FFJ is one of the patrons of 'a musical comedy entitled *The Governor*, which will be given under the auspices of the Hyoa Circle of Auxiliary No. 11, of the Stony Wold Sanatorium, at the Plaza'. Proceeds from the fundraiser are to be used 'for the support of six young women patients at the sanatorium in the Adirondacks' (*New York Herald*, 16 March 1913).

November 20 – FFJ is one of the hundreds of New York clubwomen who take part in the Thanksgiving sale 'in the east room of the Waldorf-Astoria under the auspices of Auxiliary No. 11, for the benefit of the Stony Wold Sanatorium' (*New York Herald,* 16 November 1913).

December 6 – FFJ is one of the women on duty at a booth manned by members of the New Yorkers society at the Little Mothers fair, held at the Waldorf-Astoria (*Brooklyn Daily Eagle*, 2 December 1913).

♪ 1914 July 25 – FFJ, dressed in an 'Irish lace robe with blue embroidered chiffon inset and white satin hat with paradise aigrettes', is at Hollywood Park, N.J., for the Monmouth County Horse Show Association's twenty-first annual meeting (*New York Herald,* 26 July 1914).

♪ 1915 March 17 – FFJ appears as Brünnhilde at the Euterpe Club's annual charity dinner (*New York Herald,* 18 March 1915).

May 13 – The Euterpe Club hosts a May Day luncheon at the Arrowhead Inn, Fort Washington Road. FFJ is presented with 'a gold watch bracelet as a token of appreciation of her work in the last year in the club and charity entertainments given each month' (*Musical Courier* vol. 5, issue 21, 1915, and *New York Herald*, 16 May 1915).

November 1 – FFJ attends a benefit concert at the Carnegie Hall, held by the International Music and Drama Committee and the Italian General Relief Committee, which raises $5,000 for the Italian war

effort (*New York Herald*, 2 November 1915).
December 26 – Members of the Round Table Club
hold 'a joint celebration of Christmas and observance
of the fifth anniversary of the club with a musical programme tonight at the Astor Hotel. Mrs.
Florence Foster Jenkins will be the chairman of the
programme' (*New York Herald*, 26 December 1915).
During the performance a song, *My Memory Maid,* is
dedicated to FFJ (*New York Herald*, 2 January 1916).

♪ 1916 February 1 – Mary Foster hosts a 'musicale and tea'
for the Society of Holland dames at the Biltmore
Hotel. The musical programme is arranged by FFJ,
who also performs four songs – *My Star* (Rogers), *The
Little Elfman* (music Wells; lyric Bangs), *The Spirit
Flower* (Campbell-Tipton) and *Elsa's Traum* from
Lohengrin (Wagner), accompanied by pianist Gilbert
Wilson (*New York Herald*, 6 February 1916).
March 30 – FFJ organises the musical programme for
a Euterpe Club fundraiser, featuring a performance
of the fourth act of *Rigoletto*, dancing and tableaux
– including FFJ as the Spirit of Mercy. The evening also features a 'Scarf Dance, to be given for the
first time in New York by its originator Miss Emily
Illingworth. The tableaux, arranged by Mrs. Florence
Foster Jenkins, chairman of the programme, represented a trip around the world and gave opportunities for the display of pretty costumes of many
nations. Miss Gladys Fairbanks wore robes de nuit of
various periods . . . showing the development in styles

of "nighties"' (*New York Herald*, 26 March, 31 March and 2 April 1916).

April 2 – FFJ is a guest at a luncheon given in honour of the Polish pianist Paderewski and his wife at the Biltmore Hotel (*New York Herald*, 9 April 1916).

December 2 – FFJ is one of the thousand-plus club-women involved in an American bazaar for the benefit of the work of the Little Mothers Aid Association at the Waldorf-Astoria (*New York Herald*, 26 November 1916).

December 15 – FFJ performs 'arias from *La Forza del Destino* and *Pagliacci,* with several encore songs' at a musicale and dance at the home of Mrs. J. Jones Christie in Washington Square (*New York Herald*, 17 December 1916).

♪ 1917 Date unknown – The *Musical Blue Book* runs a short biography of FFJ: 'Jenkins, Florence Foster, soprano; pianist; graduate Philadelphia Musical Academy, Heyl School of Dramatic Art, and winner Murdock Prize; editor musical department of "Expression"; Chairman of Music "Euterpe," National Round Table, etc. Res. 34 E. Thirty-second Street.'

May 17 – The Euterpe Club hold their final musical event of the season, a Men's Day with 'musical pro-gramme under the direction of Mrs. Florence Foster Jenkins, chairman of music' at the Waldorf-Astoria. FFJ also gave an address to the guests (*New York Herald,* 13 May 1917).

June 13 – Frank Jenkins dies in Milwaukee.

June 18 – The funeral for Frank Thornton Jenkins is held in Washington, D.C. He is buried at Arlington Cemetery, where his father was also buried (*Washington Post*, 19 June 1917). Florence does not attend.

August 30 – 'Mrs. Florence Foster Jenkins, daughter-in-law of the late Admiral T. Jenkins, U. S. N., gave a dinner at the Biltmore Hotel for members of the Medical Corps of the Seventh Regiment, which was followed by a musicale at the studio of Mrs. Harrison Irvine, in Carnegie Hall' (*New York Herald,* 31 August 1917).

September 3 – FFJ gives a second dinner at the Biltmore Hotel for members of the medical corps of the Seventh Regiment. 'A reception for the military men followed in the studio of Mrs. Harrison Irvine in Carnegie Hall. Patriotic songs and choruses by the guests and solos by Mrs. Jenkins, soprano' (*New York Herald*, 9 September 1917).

Date unknown (around September) – FFJ founds the Verdi Club, 'incorporated to encourage music, litera-ture and art'. Florence is the club's President: Mrs. Rose M Cottolle is installed as a director (*Brooklyn Daily Eagle*, 3 October 1917).

November 14 – FFJ and St. Clair Bayfield are among the guests at a 'musicale and reception' given in the studio home of the singer Astofolo Pescia (*Musical Courier*, 22 November 1917).

November 28 – FFJ and St. Clair Bayfield move to 66

West 37th Street (date recorded in St. Clair's diary), into rented rooms above the showroom of the Mascot Talking Machine Mfg. Co. FFJ is reported to have taken over the lease on the rooms in *The Sun* (New York), 22 October 1917.

November 28 – The Verdi Club hosts its first morning musicale. 'One aim of the new club is to do honor to the genius of Verdi. Another object of the club is to assist the war fund, the entire proceeds from the club events being devoted to the American Red Cross' (*New York Herald,* 18 November 1917).

December 1 – FFJ is one of the 'more than one thousand young women and matrons' who take part in the American Bazaar, held at the Waldorf-Astoria to raise funds for the Little Mother's Aid Association (*New York Herald,* 25 November 1917).

December 7 – The Verdi Club gives 'a musicale and dramatic afternoon' at the Waldorf-Astoria, New York. A fundraiser for the American Red Cross, the musical programme features a selection of 'Indian songs', including one – *Red Day* – dedicated to FFJ, plus a one-act play, a dramatic reading and an 'oriental dance by Little Dolores' (*New York Herald*, 2 December 1917).

♪ 1918   January 4 – The New Yorkers club holds its annual musicale at the Hotel Astor. FFJ is chairman of the day, and the event raises funds for war relief work (*The Sun* (New York), 6 January 1918).

January 9 – The Verdi Club 'begins its New Year

program' at the Waldorf-Astoria. Musicians include three guests from the Metropolitan Opera House and the Verdi Club's own string quartet (*The Sun* (New York), 6 January 1918).

February 15 – The Verdi Club holds a 'musical and dramatic afternoon' at the Waldorf-Astoria. Mary Foster is among the guests attending (*New York Herald,* 10 February 1918).

March 6 – FFJ is presented with 'large silk Italian and American flags' at a meeting of the Verdi Club at the Waldorf-Astoria. 'Mr. Carlo Edwards, in a brief speech, expressed the esteem in which Mrs. Jenkins is held' (*New York Herald*, 10 March 1918).

April 11 – The ballroom of New York's Waldorf-Astoria Hotel is adorned with 'thousands of silver skylarks on a sky of Italian blue with green decorations suggesting the woods of spring' for the Verdi Club's Ball of the Silver Skylarks. President and founder FFJ is 'presented with a golden laurel wreath surrounding a lyre of gold to which was attached an enamelled shield of red and gray, the colors of the club' (*The Sun* (New York), 21 April 1918).

April 17 – FFJ is in Washington, D.C., as a delegate to the Daughters of the American Revolution conference (*New York Herald*, 21 April 1918).

August 17 – FFJ performs at a benefit for the Larchmont Red Cross at the Belvedere Hotel, Larchmont Manor. 'The program included duets and solos by Mrs. Florence Foster Jenkins and Pedro

Guetary, accompanied by Mrs. Harrison Irvine'
(*Brooklyn Daily Eagle*, 18 August 1918). The benefit
raised $200 (*New York Herald*, 19 August 1918).
August 21 – FFJ sends a basket of roses from the
Verdi Club to Enrico Caruso and his wife, honey-
mooning at the Knickerbocker Hotel, New York
(*New York Herald*, 22 August 1918).
September 16 – FFJ, representing the Verdi Club,
is one of more than twenty clubwomen at a meeting
held at the Waldorf-Astoria 'for the purpose of com-
bining their efforts in a strong campaign to aid the
Fourth Liberty Loan drive. They also will combine
for American Red Cross work and other war relief'
(*New York Herald*, 22 September 1918).
December 5 – FFJ is one of the featured soloists
performing at a Verdi Club musicale at the Waldorf-
Astoria (*New York Herald*, 8 December 1918).

♪ 1919 March 5 – 'Caruso Day' is celebrated by the Verdi
Club at the Waldorf-Astoria. Caruso 'has sent a large
photograph of himself, autographed and inscribed
with his compliments, to the club. Copies of it will
be presented as souvenirs to the members of the club'
(*New York Herald*, 2 March 1919).
April 9 – The Verdi Club's Ball of the Silver
Skylarks at the at the Waldorf-Astoria features
Melville Charlton, who conducts a performance
of *Il Trovatore*, featuring vocalists from the Boston
Grand Opera Company and players from the New
York Symphony (*New York Age*, 19 April 1919). Mrs.

Charles Dorrance Foster (FFJ's mother) is listed as a patron (*The Sun* (New York), 6 April 1919).

May 24 – 'Mrs. Florence Foster Jenkins, of the Hotel Seymour, West Forty-Fourth Street, has returned from Washington, where she was a delegate of the Daughters of the American Revolution at the recent convention of the order' (*New York Herald*, 25 May 1919).

August – 'Mrs. Florence Foster Jenkins, of New York, president of the Verdi Society, who was at Massasoit for the snow ball, went to Newport, where she sang at a private musicale. Mrs. Jenkins has been invited to sing at St. Peter's by the Sea on her return' (*New York Herald*, 17 August 1919).

October 2 – The Verdi Club holds a benefit performance at the Garrick Theatre, New York for the Italian Red Cross. St. Clair appears, performing in scenes from *Twelfth Night* and *The Melting Pot* (*New York Times*, 2 October 1919).

November 5 – FFJ, 'founder and president of the Verdi Club, was greeted by an overflowing audience at its morning musicale' at the Waldorf-Astoria, New York (*Musical Courier*, 20 November 1919).

December 12 – The Verdi Club hosts a musicale at the Waldorf-Astoria, New York. FFJ is presented with 'a beautiful hand-made vanity bag, matching [her] handsome hat and gown'. St. Clair gives a speech: FFJ is honoured with 'a eulogistic poem' (*Musical Courier*, 1 January 1920).

December 23 – 'The Verdi Club, Florence Foster Jenkins founder and president, gave an hour of music at the Playland Exhibition' in New York's Grand Central Palace, featuring Thelma Thelmaire (soprano) and Ronald Allan (tenor). 'Florence Foster Jenkins herself accompanied all the soloists' (*Musical Courier,* 8 January 1920).

♪ 1920 Date unknown – Cosme McMoon moves to New York.

January 7 – FFJ is the pianist for Marbella Armand (cellist) and Ronald Allan (tenor) at a luncheon and musicale given by the National Patriotic Society in the banquet hall of the McAlpin Hotel (*Musical Courier,* 22 January 1920).

January 14 – Verdi Club luncheon, followed by a tea for 'around 500 members of the club'. Mrs. Charles Dorrance Foster (FFJ's mother) is guest of honour (*Musical Courier*, 1 January 1920).

March 1 – FFJ gives a speech at a dinner, held at Keen's restaurant, 45th Street, given by the Dramatic Arts Club (*The Billboard*, 5 March 1920).

March 3 – The Verdi Club hosts a musical morning at the Waldorf-Astoria (*The Sun and New York Herald,* 22 February 1920). A song, *Dreamy Eyes* by Arthur Gollnik, is debuted and dedicated to the club (*Musical Courier,* 18 March 1920).

April 13 – The Verdi Club hosts its Arabian Nights-themed fourth annual Ball of the Silver Skylarks. Enrico Caruso is listed as head of the 'advisory board'. FFJ appears, in costume, as Scheherazade; St. Clair as an Arabian prince. Over a thousand people attend (*The Sun and New York Herald,* 18 April 1920). April 14 – FFJ's 'friends gave her a breakfast after the grand concert and ball of the Verdi Club' (*Musical Courier,* 22 April 1920).

May 19 – The Verdi Club gives a 'springtime luncheon and revels' in the roof garden of the Hotel Astor. FFJ's vocal coach, Seismit-Doda, is listed as one of the performers (*Musical Courier,* 13 May 1920).

♪ 1921 January 14 – FFJ directs the musical content for the New Yorkers Club meeting. Musicians include violinist Mozelle Bennett (*Musical Courier,* 10 February 1921).

February 14 – The second annual Verdi Club benefit is held at the Garrick Theatre. St. Clair directs a performance of *Twelfth Night*; proceeds to the Italian Red Cross (*Evening World* (New York), 4 February 1921).

February 15 – FFJ gives a tea and musicale for the cast and crew of *Twelfth Night* at the MacDowell Club. St. Clair is in attendance (*New York Tribune*, 20 February 1921).

March 2 – The Verdi Club hosts a morning musicale at the Waldorf-Astoria (*New York Tribune,* 27 February 1921). FFJ presents a pearl necklace to Miss Estelle Christie, Chairman of Arrangements, and an ostrich feather fan to Mrs. Arthur H. Bridge,

Chairman of the Ways and Means Committee (*New York Tribune*, 20 March 1921).

April 20 – FFJ appears as 'the Sun Goddess' during a tableau at the Verdi Club's fourth annual ball of the Silver Skylarks at the Waldorf-Astoria (*Brooklyn Daily Eagle*, 22 April 1921).

May 11 – The Verdi Club holds its annual luncheon at the Waldorf-Astoria (*Musical Courier,* 12 May 1921). St. Clair gives a talk: 'Up-to-the-minute Recollections of a Season at the Belasco Theatre with Deburau'.

May – FFJ is reported as having $15.50 in unclaimed funds in the Girard Trust Co, of Philadelphia, which she needs to either withdraw or forfeit (*Philadelphia Enquirer,* 18 & 20 May 1921).

June 1 – The Verdi Club holds a musical afternoon at the Hotel McAlpin. 'A talk on art' is given by the sculptor Lily C. Mayer, who also unveiled a bust of Verdi that she presented to the club (*Musical Courier,* 2 June 1921).

November 9 – The Verdi Club holds a 'Caruso memorial musicale'. 'Aldo Randegger played a newly-composed funeral march, and Miss Adele Chester Deming presented a poem written for the occasion, entitled "Caruso".' (*New York Tribune*, 13 November 1921).

December 16 – The Verdi Club hosts 'a musical and dramatic afternoon' at the Waldorf-Astoria (*New York Tribune*, 11 December 1921) Guests are given printed copies of Adele Chester's *Caruso* poem.

♪ 1922 February 10 – A Musical and Dramatic Afternoon
is given by the Verdi Club, FFJ president, at the
Waldorf-Astoria. 'The "Miniature", a one act play by
Walter Frith, will be produced under the direction
of St. Clair Bayfield. Those in the cast are Catherine
Sayre, St. Clair Bayfield, Miss Winifred Johnstone
and George Riddell. A feature of the musical pro-
gram will be the introduction of the Verdi Club Trio,
whose members are Mozelle Bennett, violin; Flavie
Van den Hende, cello, and Rosalie Heller Klein,
piano' (*New York Tribune*, 5 February 1922).
August 16 – St. Clair produces Shakespeare's *A
Midsummer Night's Dream* at the Larchmont Yacht
Club. Funds raised go towards the establishment of
the Larchmont Free Library. FFJ is listed as a patron
(*New York Tribune*, 17 August 1922).
November 8 – At a Verdi Club 'soiree dansante' at
the MacDowell Club, FFJ sings from *Romeo and
Juliet* and 'a group of French songs' accompanied by
violinist Guido Villetti of the Metropolitan Opera
Company, and 'was so vociferously and continu-
ally applauded that she had to add encores' (*Musical
Courier*, 23 November 1922).
November 19 – FFJ performs solo at a gala Naval
Night at the Pleiades Club, Hotel Brevoort in
Greenwich Village, New York: 'Commander Charles
A. Adams was the toastmaster, and besides the distin-
guished members, including admirals, commanders
and captains, who made addresses, a musical program

was given' (*Musical Courier,* 23 November 1922).
December 8 – At a Verdi Club musicale to celebrate
the organisation's fifth anniversary, St. Clair adapts
and appears in the one-act play *The Ninth Waltz.* FFJ
receives several letters from well-wishers (*Musical
Courier,* 22 December 1922).

♪ 1923 February 9 – The Verdi Club presents a one-act play,
A Little Fowl Play, adapted and produced by St. Clair
Bayfield (FFJ scrapbook, NYPL [New York Public
Library]).
March 15 – 'The tasteful cover design on the title-
page of the sixteen-page program of the Verdi Club,
with its colorful illustrations of Verdi and operatic
heroes, the poet Shelley, the muses, etc. (from a sketch
of President Florence Foster Jenkins, by Annabel
Krebs Culverwell), augured an interesting evening
at the Waldorf-Astoria grand ballroom.' FFJ appears
in a tableau vivant as The Snow Queen. 'Then Mr.
Adams (author of two poems in her praise printed
in the program) presented her with a handsome
velvet box, which was later found to contain a beautiful platinum wrist-watch, set with at least fifty
diamonds, the gift of the members. Blushing becom-
ingly, President Jenkins accepted with modesty'
(*Musical Courier*, 22 March 1923).
October – 'The birthday of Giuseppe Verdi was celebrated recently by the Verdi Club of New York City
when the club presented to the city two blue spruce
trees twelve feet high, which were planted on either

side of the Verdi statue which stands in a triangular
park at the intersection of 72nd Street and Broadway.
Mrs. Florence Foster Jenkins, president of the
Verdi club, had a prominent part in the ceremonies,
which were attended by a distinguished audience'
(*Amsterdam Evening Recorder,* 20 October 1923).
December 8 – The Verdi Club presents a one-act
play, *The Ninth Waltz*, adapted and produced by
St. Clair Bayfield (FFJ scrapbook, NYPL).

♪ 1924 January – 'The Verdi Club, which is one of the
largest musical clubs in the city, will give Handel's
"Messiah" in January at the Ritz-Carlton, and Miss
Grace Liddane will be the soloist at the presentation of this oratorio' (*Amsterdam Evening Recorder,* 20
October 1923).
March 19 – The seventh annual Verdi Club Ball is
held at the Waldorf-Astoria ballroom. 'Tableaux
vivants completed the program. After a few
moment's wait there appeared, standing on the stage
rocks, the imposing figure of President Florence
Foster Jenkins as Brunhilde, with shining silver
spear, shield of gold, and white robe, with the big
helmet hat. Loud applause and bravos caused the
curtain to show her thus posed some six times' (FFJ
scrapbook, NYPL).
December 5 – The Verdi Club presents a one-act
play, *The Counsel's Opinion*, with St. Clair Bayfield as
Sir John Bendwill, K.C. (FFJ scrapbook, NYPL).

♪ 1925 January 19 – FFJ appears in a New Yorkers society
musicale at the Astor Hotel. 'The chairman of music,
Mrs. Florence Foster Jenkins, will present the program, including piano solos by Gladys Barnett; songs
by Florence Foster Jenkins; harp solos by Arthur
Jones' (*Brooklyn Daily Eagle,* 17 January 1925).

♪ 1926 January 6 – FFJ is one of '150 presidents of the
foremost clubs of New York and Brooklyn' invited
to a President's day musicale given at the Waldorf-
Astoria by the Rubenstein Club (*Brooklyn Standard
Union,* 3 January 1926).

♪ 1927 February 22 – FFJ performs for the Washington
Headquarters Association at celebrations for the
195th anniversary of George Washington's birth
(*New York Times*, 20 February 1927).
May 8 – According to a report in the *Morning
Telegraph*, FFJ 'is very busy and has already sung at
more than twenty occasions this season'.

♪ 1928 Date unknown – FFJ meets Edwin McArthur and
engages him as her main accompanist.
September 4 – 'Mrs. Florence Foster Jenkins, president of the Verdi club of New York City, is spending the week in Amsterdam and will coach, with
her teacher, Miss Grace M. Liddane, in preparation
for the annual recital which Mrs. Jenkins will give
October 30 in the grand ballroom of the Ritz-Carlton'
(*Amsterdam Evening Recorder,* 4 September 1928).

♪ **1929** March 20 – The Verdi Club stage the opera *Othello*
at this year's Ball of the Silver Skylarks, at the
Waldorf-Astoria Hotel. Funds raised go to benefit
the Veteran's Mountain Camp in the Adirondack
Mountains (*Daily Star, Queensborough,* 21 March
1929).

August – FFJ 'recently had a musicale at her suite
in the Hotel Seymour. Maude Beard accompanied
Madame in a group of German and English songs'
(*Musical Courier,* 30 August 1929).

♪ **1930** Date unknown – FFJ meets Cosme McMoon and
engages him as pianist. At first he plays alongside McArthur; in 1933 he replaces McArthur and
becomes FFJ's main accompanist.

September/October – FFJ appears 'in New Rochelle
as soprano soloist in a request program of mod-
ern French songs for the Women's Club of New
Rochelle. Her interpretation and diction were favour-
ably commented upon as showing careful training
and her voice was praised for its limpid quality'
(*Yonkers Statesman,* 27 October 1930).

October 29 – FFJ gives her annual song recital at
the Ritz-Carlton Hotel accompanied by Edwin
McArthur. Cosme McMoon plays piano solos (FFJ
scrapbook, NYPL).

November 7 – Mary Hoagland Foster dies at the
Park Central Hotel, New York (*New York Times,* 8
November 1930).

November 9 – The funeral of Mary Foster is held at

Campbell's Funeral Church, 6th St and Broadway
(*New York Times*, 8 November 1930).

December 3 – FFJ performs at a meeting of the
Patriotic Women of America at the Plaza Hotel (*New
York Times*, 27 November 1930).

♪ 1931 March 9 – FFJ gives a luncheon in honour of the
Baroness von Hindenburg, niece of Paul von
Hindenburg the German president, at the Ritz
Tower. St. Clair is among the guests (*The Sun* (New
York), 10 March 1931).

April 7 – FFJ, on behalf of the Verdi Club, presents
soprano Gina Pinnera with a gold medal, inscribed
'for the most wonderful natural voice of the present day'. Baroness von Hindenburg is also present
(inscription on press photograph: Bettman Collection,
Corbis).

September 17 – FFJ performs in Newport, Rhode
Island: 'A concert was given at the Historical Society
rooms by Florence Foster Jenkins, soprano, of New
York, assisted by Leila Hearne Cannes, pianist' (*New
York Times*, 18 September 1931). Edwin McArthur
is also present. One of the songs performed is a new
arrangement of the *Blue Danube Waltz* by Cosme
McMoon: the encore is *Clavelitos*, complete with
'scattering flowers in Spanish style'. 'Her voice is of
good quality, flexible, even throughout a good range'
(*Newport Mercury*, 25 November 1931).

September 30 – FFJ and Cosme are guests at a dinner given by Mr. and Mrs. H. Winfield Chapin at

their home in Syracuse (*Syracuse American*, 4 October 1931).

♪ 1932 June – 'Florence Foster Jenkins was the vocalist at the poetry week meeting at the St. Regis Hotel, New York, recently. Edwin McArthur accompanied. Her program included songs by Reger and Strauss and a vocal arrangement of the *Blue Danube Waltz*, specially written for her by Cosmo McMoon [sic], remembered as her accompanist in a Syracuse recital' (*Syracuse American,* 19 June 1932).

July 24 – 'Mrs. Florence Foster Jenkins gave a party at the Seymour Hotel in celebration of her birthday. The guests included Fortuno Gallo, Mme. Gina Pinnera, Mme. Nana Genovese, Mr. and Mrs. Edwin McArthur, Mr. and Mrs. Guido Ciccolini, Miss Betsie Spogen, St. Clair Bayfield. Mr. and Mrs. Harry Baum and Charles Hunt Parker' (*The Sun* (New York)*,* 28 July 1932). St. Clair's diary notes that FFJ is Charlie Parker's godmother.

September 8 – FFJ gives a return performance at the Historical Society rooms in Newport, Rhode Island, accompanied by Leila Hearne Cannes and Edwin McArthur. Songs include *The Virgin's Slumber Song*, plus works by Strauss, Verdi, Liszt and Schubert (FFJ scrapbook, NYPL).

October 5 – FFJ is guest of honour at a meeting of the Children's Museum Auxiliary Education Committee. She gave a talk entitled 'The Value of the Spoken Word' (*Brooklyn Daily Eagle,* 6 October 1932).

♪ 1933   March 15 – The Verdi Club hosts its annual Ball of
the Silver Skylarks. FFJ appears, in one of the tableaux vivants, as Madame Dubarry (FFJ scrapbook,
NYPL).

May – 'Florence Foster Jenkins, founder-president
of the Verdi Club and president of the American
Pen Women, New York, sang recently as guest of
honor at the authors breakfast, Stoneleigh Court,
Washington' (*Syracuse American,* 28 May 1933).

May 24 – FFJ gives a recital at the St. Regis Hotel for
poetry week (*Syracuse American,* 28 May 1933).

July – FFJ, accompanied by Cosme McMoon and
violinist Anja Sinayeff, sings a group of French songs
at the home of Mrs. John E. White in New York
(*Syracuse American,* 23 July 1933).

August 17 – FFJ performs a selection of songs by
up-and-coming New York composers at Sherry's,
300 Park Avenue, at 2:30 pm. Songwriters include
Florence Mallory Peyton, Frederick Shattuck and
Cosme McMoon. St. Clair Bayfield gives a recitation
(*New York Times*, 16 August 1933).

November 2 – FFJ's annual recital at the Ritz-
Carlton, accompanied by the Pascarella String
Quartet. She performs her own composition *Trysting
Time* (*New York Times*, 29 October 1933).

December 11 – FFJ is a guest at a tea given by Mrs.
Theodore Roosevelt, widow of the late President, at
the Roosevelt house, 28 East 20th Street, New York
City (*Herald Statesman, Yonkers,* 13 December 1933).

December 18 – FFJ performs at a meeting of the Society of New York State Women at Sherry's, Park Avenue, Manhattan (*Brooklyn Daily Eagle*, 17 December 1933).

♪ 1934 January 17 – Florence Darnault's bust of Verdi unveiled at ceremony at the Plaza Hotel (*New York Evening Post*, 18 January 1934). Darnault discovers FFJ's secret: that she is bald.

March 14 – Annual Ball of the Silver Skylarks: FFJ appears in a tableau vivant as Catherine the Great. St. Clair presents two one-act plays: *Paris of the Golden Apple* and *Romance of '76,* and selections from the opera *Othello* are performed (FFJ scrapbook, NYPL).

July – FFJ retires as president of the New York branch of the League of American Penwomen. The article confirms that 'during the last year she sang at 50 concerts' (*Wilkes-Barre Record,* 13 July 1934).

September 5 – FFJ gives her annual recital at the Newport Historical Society. Her accompanist is Mrs. Armistead (*The Sun* (New York), 5 September 1934). November 8 – FFJ's annual recital at the Ritz-Carlton, once again accompanied by the Pascarella String Quartet (*New York Times*, 4 November 1934).

♪ 1935 January 16 – FFJ performs, accompanied by William Cowdrey, organist of the First Congregational Church, at a luncheon given by the National Society Patriotic Women of America at the Hotel Commodore, Manhattan. She also directs the day's music programme (*Brooklyn Daily Eagle*, 13 January 1935).

October 30 – Annual recital in the Ritz-Carlton Hotel ballroom, with pianist Nathan Price. Songs include *The Bell Song*; Cosme McMoon accompanied her in two of his own works. Parts of the recital are filmed (FFJ scrapbook, NYPL).

December 4 – FFJ gives a presentation at a meeting of the National Society of Patriotic Women at the Hotel Plaza (*New York Times*, 1 December 1935).

December 13 – The Verdi Club holds a musical and dramatic afternoon at the Hotel Plaza. Cosme plays several of his own compositions; St. Clair adapts, produces and appears in a one-act version of Mary, Queen of Scots, and 'a moving picture of Mme. Jenkins' Concert given at the Ritz-Carlton, October 30th, will be shown. Come and see yourself as you appear in a moving picture and bring your friends to hear one of the best programs of the winter' (FFJ scrapbook, NYPL).

♪ 1936 October 29 – Annual recital in the Ritz-Carlton Hotel ballroom, with the Pascarella Chamber Music Society (*New York Times*, 25 October 1936).

♪ 1937 January 14 – Recital at the Ritz-Carlton Hotel, with pianists Almero Albanesi and Cosme McMoon (FFJ scrapbook, NYPL).

April 11 – FFJ gives a recital at the Ritz-Carlton (FFJ scrapbook, NYPL).

April 18 – Recital at the Mayflower Hotel in Washington, D.C., accompanied by Willa Semple (FFJ scrapbook, NYPL).

May 25 – FFJ gives recital in honour of Poetry Week at Sherry's, accompanied by Cosme McMoon. Programme includes the McMoon/Jenkins-composed song *Trysting Time* (FFJ scrapbook, NYPL).

November 3 – Annual recital at the Ritz-Carlton Hotel, assisted by the Pascarella Chamber Music Society (*Brooklyn Daily Eagle*, 31 October 1937). The set includes Cosme McMoon's song *Gypsy Fantasy*.

December 7 – FFJ is photographed at the Park Hill Community Club, where the Chaminade Club are holding their annual president's day (*Herald Statesman, Yonkers,* 8 December 1937).

♪ 1938 March 4 – FFJ gives a performance for New York State Women at Sherry's, with Cosme McMoon accompanying (FFJ scrapbook, NYPL).

April – FFJ gives a concert in Queens, at the home of Thomas H. Grafenreid, in front of two hundred people, accompanied by Cosme McMoon (FFJ scrapbook, NYPL).

May – FFJ begins a series of Sunday afternoon recitals for radio station WINS (*The Musician: America's Leading Magazine for Musicians, Music-lovers, Teachers and Students*, vols 44-45, 1939).

September – FFJ sings at a recital in Pittsburgh (*The Musician,* October 1938).

October – FFJ appears in concert at the Newport

Historical Society (*The Musician,* October 1938).

October 12 – FFJ sings at the Westchester Biltmore Club (FFJ scrapbook, NYPL).

October 27 – Annual recital at the Ritz-Carlton Hotel, with Cosme McMoon (*New York Times*, 27 October 1938).

December 9 – A bust of FFJ is unveiled at the Hotel Plaza: 'The unveiling and presentation of a bust of Mrs. Florence Foster Jenkins, founder and president of the Verdi Club, was a feature of the musical and dramatic program of the club in the grand ballroom of the Hotel Plaza'. Cosme plays (*New York Times*, 10 December 1938).

♪ 1939 January 15 – FFJ (listed in the newspaper as 'Lady Florence Jenkins') and St. Clair perform at a musical afternoon at the Royalton Hotel, Manhattan (*Brooklyn Daily Eagle,* 15 January 1939).

February 18 – FFJ gives a talk, in her role as president of the National Society of Patriotic Women of America, at a 'patriotic meeting' held by the State democratic Forum at the Hotel Peter Stuyvesant, NY (*Brooklyn Daily Eagle,* 12 February 1939).

March – FFJ engaged by the Hungarian Chamber of Commerce to perform in an evening of Hungarian songs at Carnegie Hall (*The Musician*, 1939).

April 20 – FFJ gives a recital in Washington, D.C., accompanied by Malton Boyce and Olga Biber. 'Appearing in a Hungarian national costume for her closing group, wearing a picturesque hairdress [sic] studded with flowers, Mrs. Jenkins ... transported her audience into a far-away country.' Material included *Gypsy Fantasie* by Cosme McMoon and *Brook*, written for FFJ by Elmer Russ (*Evening Star* (Washington), 21 April 1939).

May 16 – FFJ gives a 'theatre party' in honour of St. Clair at the Biltmore Theatre, Manhattan (*Brooklyn Daily Eagle,* 14 May 1939).

May 24 – FFJ and St. Clair attend an engagement party given by Mr. and Mrs. Lewis Dana Knowlton of Hudson View Gardens, Manhattan (*Brooklyn Daily Eagle,* 25 May 1939).

June 24 – Members of the Verdi Club present 'America on Review' as part of a 'Merrie England'-style pageant and dinner at the New York World's Fair (*Brooklyn Daily Eagle,* 24 June 1939).

September 7 – FFJ gives a song recital at the Newport Historical Society; her pianist is William J. Cowdrey (*New York Times*, 8 September 1939). A poster advertising this performance exists in the FFJ archive in the New York Public Library.

October 26 – FFJ's annual recital at the Ritz-Carlton, accompanied by Cosme McMoon. Songs include *Queen of the Night, Clavelitos* and *Serenata Mexicana* (FFJ scrapbook, NYPL).

December 18 – The Manhattan Study Club hold a Christmas Song recital at Sherry's, New York. 'Mme. Florence Foster Jenkins will sing the program ... Mme. Jenkins will sing with flute obbligato played

by Louis Alberghini. A special song written by Grace
Bush will be sung. St. Clair Bayfield will recite.
Cosme McMoon will be the accompanist of the after-
noon' (*Brooklyn Daily Eagle*, 17 December 1939).

♪ 1940 February 14 – FFJ, in her role as president of the
National Society of Patriotic Women of America,
hosts a luncheon at the Hotel Commodore. Sculptor
Florence Darnault and St. Clair Bayfield are among
the guest speakers (*Brooklyn Daily Eagle*, 11 February
1940).
March 7 – At this year's Ball of the Silver Skylarks
selections from *Faust* are performed. FFJ appears in
tableaux (FFJ scrapbook, NYPL).
November 7 – FFJ gives her annual recital at the
Ritz-Carlton ballroom, accompanied by Cosme
McMoon. Programme includes *Charmant Oiseau,
Valse Caressante* and *Musical Snuff Box* (FFJ scrapbook, NYPL).

♪ 1941 April 10 – FFJ sings at the Washington Club (FFJ
scrapbook, NYPL).
March 6 – At the annual Ball of the Silver Skylarks,
FFJ appears in Spanish costume. Selections from
Pagliacci are performed (FFJ scrapbook, NYPL).
May – FFJ enters Melotone Recording Studios for the
first time, recording at least two songs, *The Bell Song*
(Delibes) and the *Queen of the Night* aria.
June 16 – *Queen of the Night* is reviewed in *Time*
magazine.

October 30 – 'Those Who Know will be interested in the announcement by Mme. Florence Foster Jenkins that she will give another of her highly individual song recitals at the Ritz-Carlton Hotel on Thursday evening' (*The Sun* (New York), 2 October 1941).

♪ 1942 March 5 – At the annual Ball of the Silver Skylarks, FFJ performs, with Cosme, in her Angel of Inspiration costume (FFJ scrapbook, NYPL). November 24 – FFJ appears in a 'Song Celebration' with others including Leon Rothier, Henry Harrison and C.D. Batchelor at the Hotel Wellington. The programme celebrates the 2,000th performance of Elmo Russ's song *America Forever Free* (*New York Times*, 24 November 1942).

♪ 1943 April 15 – Recital in Washington, accompanied by pianist Malton Boyce. Songs include *Biassy, Adele's Laughing Song* and *Gypsy Fantasie*, a song that Cosme McMoon has dedicated to FFJ. She also performs *Trailing Arbutus* (FFJ scrapbook, NYPL). November 4 – FFJ's annual recital at the Ritz-Carlton ballroom. Songs include *The Bell Song, Charmant Oiseau, Like a Bird* and *Valse Caressante* (*New York Daily Mirror*, 5 November 1943).

♪ 1944 February 4 – Recital at Sherry's for the Society of New York State Women, accompanied by Cosme McMoon. The performance includes *The Bell Song, Charmant Oiseau, Like a Bird* and *Valse Caressante* (FFJ scrapbook, NYPL).

October 17 – 'Raymond Scott, who once wrote
a screwball operatic selection for sopranos called
"Lesson In Arithmetic" is penning a special number
for the Carnegie Hall concert of Florence Foster
Jenkins, whose vocal efforts were once described by
a music critic as sounding like "a cuckoo in its cups"'
(*Philadelphia Enquirer,* 17 October 1944).
October 25 – FFJ makes her now-legendary appear-
ance at Carnegie Hall, accompanied by Cosme
McMoon. The audience includes Cole Porter,
Lily Pons, Gypsy Rose Lee and actress Tallulah
Bankhead.
October 29/30 – FFJ has a heart attack while shop-
ping at a music store in New York.
November 26 – FFJ dies at the Hotel Seymour, New
York, 'after an illness of three weeks' (*New York
Times*, 27 November 1944).

♪ 1945 January 28 – Irving Johnson's article, 'Discordant
Diva's Missing Will', appears in *American Weekly*
magazine.

♪ 1946 January 27 – St. Clair Bayfield and Kathleen 'Kay'
Weatherly marry at St. Stephen's Episcopal Church,
West 69th Street (St. Clair Bayfield Diary, 1946).

♪ 1954 April 12 – RCA records release *A Florence! Foster!!
Jenkins!!! Recital!!!!* Cosme records an interview with
Chick Crumpacker, which is issued to radio stations
to help promote the album.

♪ 1967 May 19 – St. Clair Bayfield dies in New York.

♪ 1980 August 22 – Cosme McMoon dies, of pancreatic cancer, in San Antonio, Texas.

♪ 1987 24 February – Edwin McArthur dies, after giving a piano lesson, at his studio in Hackensack, New Jersey (*New York Times,* 25 February 1987).

A Florence! Foster!! Jenkins!!! Discography!!!!

MELOTONE RELEASES (ALL UNNUMBERED)

Florence Foster Jenkins, Cosme McMoon (piano): Delibes: Lakmé – Bell Song. 10" single-sided shellac disc.

Florence Foster Jenkins, Cosme McMoon (piano): Mozart: Die Zauberflote – Aria of the Queen of the Night (Act 2)/McMoon: Serenata Mexicana. 12" double-sided shellac disc.

Florence Foster Jenkins, Cosme McMoon (piano): Strauss: Die Fledermaus – Adele's laughing Song/Bach: Biassy (based on Prelude No. XVI; words by Pushkin). 12" double-sided shellac disc.

Florence Foster Jenkins, with flute and piano accompaniment, Cosme McMoon (piano), Louis Alberghini (flute): David: Charmant Oiseau (from 'Perle du Brésil'. 10" double-sided shellac disc (song split over two sides).

Florence Foster Jenkins, Cosme McMoon (piano): Valse Caressante. 10" double-sided shellac disc (song split into two, neither side given lead status).

Florence Foster Jenkins, Cosme McMoon (piano): Delibes: Lakmé – Bell Song/Liadoff – Musical Snuff Box & McMoon

– Like a Bird (words by Madame Jenkins). 12" double-sided shellac disc (posthumous reissue).

The original Melotone releases came with typewritten labels, usually with details in black and 'FLORENCE FOSTER JENKINS' in red. Later issues (circa 1945/6) came with fully printed labels, with text in blue. The Melotone releases were available until 1954. Some of the later, posthumous, pressings came with a free twelve-page booklet, *Florence Foster Jenkins, An Appreciation*, written by Milton Bendiner for Melotone.

   Valse Caressante was issued posthumously, although it is more than likely that a few acetate copies were pressed immediately after it was recorded. It does not appear on any of the RCA collections, nor is it included in the 'official' discography that appears in *Florence Foster Jenkins, An Appreciation*.

1954

RCA LRT-7000: *A Florence! Foster!! Jenkins!!! Recital!!!!* (US)
   Side One: Mozart – Aria: Queen of the Night (from The Magic Flute)/ Liadoff – The Musical Snuff-Box (lyrics by [English version] Adele Epstein)/ McMoon – Like a Bird (words by Mme. Jenkins)/ Delibes – Bell Song (from Lakmé)/ McMoon – Serenata Mexicana
   Side Two: David – Charmant Oiseau (from Pearl of Brazil)/ Bach, Pavlovich – Biassy (words by Pushkin)/ Johann Strauss, Jr. – Adele's Laughing Song (from Die Fledermaus) (lyrics by [English version] Lorraine Noel Finley)
10", 33$\frac{1}{3}$ rpm; also available as a double 7" EP set

1956

HMV 7EB 6022 (UK): *Florence Foster Jenkins* (EP)
  Side One: The Queen of the Night Aria/ Biassy
  Side Two: Adele's Laughing Song/ Like a Bird
7", 45 rpm

1959

RCA RCX-157 (UK): *Florence Foster Jenkins* (EP)
  Side One: The Queen of the Night Aria/ Biassy
  Side Two: Adele's Laughing Song/ Like a Bird
[Reissue of 7EB 6022 with different sleeve]
7", 45 rpm

1962

RCA LM-2597 (UK, US, Europe): *The Glory (????) of the
Human Voice*
  Side One: Queen of the Night Aria (Der Hölle Rache)/ The
  Musical Snuff-Box/ Like a Bird/ Bell Song (Glöckchenarie)/
  Charmant Oiseau/ Biassy/ Adele's Laughing Song (Mein
  Herr Marquis)
  Side Two: A Faust Travesty (not by FFJ).
12" LP

1970

RCA International INT 1150 (UK): *The Unbelievable Glory of
the Human Voice*
  Side One: Queen of the Night Aria/ The Musical Snuff-
  Box/ Like a Bird/ Bell Song/ Charmant Oiseau/ Biassy/
  Adele's Laughing Song

Side Two: A Faust Travesty (not by FFJ).
[Reissue of LM-2597 with different sleeve]
12" LP

1988
Legendary Recordings LR 213 (Europe): *The Incomparable Diva: Florence Foster Jenkins and her Disputed Rivals*
    Side One: McMoon – Serenata Mexicana/ (other songs not by FFJ).
12" LP

1992
RCA Red Seal GK 61175: *The Glory (????) of the Human Voice*
    Queen of the Night Aria/ The Musical Snuff-Box/ Like a Bird/ Bell Song/ Serenata Mexicana/ Charmant Oiseau/ Biassy/ Adele's Laughing Song/ A Faust Travesty (not FFJ).
CD

2003
Naxos 8120711 (UK/Europe): *Florence Foster Jenkins and Friends: Murder on the High C's*
    Queen of the Night Aria/ Serenata Mexicana/ The Musical Snuff-Box/ Like a Bird/ Bell Song/ Charmant Oiseau/ Adele's Laughing Song/ Biassy/ Valse Caressante/ (other songs not by FFJ).
CD
[This is the first release to collect all nine of FFJ's extant recordings together.]

2004

Membran Music Ltd 222078-205 (UK/Europe): *The Nightingale: Der Hölle Rache*

    Adele's Laughing Song/ Queen of the Night Aria/ Biassy/ The Musical Snuff-Box/ Like a Bird/ Bell Song/ Valentine's Aria (from A Faust Travesty, not FFJ)/ Charmant Oiseau

CD

Homophone 1001 (US): *The Muse Surmounted: Florence Foster Jenkins and 11 of Her Rivals*

    McMoon – Valse Caressante/ Cosme McMoon – Reminiscence of Florence Foster Jenkins (Interview with Cosme McMoon)/ (other songs not by FFJ).

CD

[Compiled by Gregor Benko.]

2005

Documents/Meisterwerke/Membran 222078 (UK/Europe): *The Nightingale – Der Hölle Rache*

    Adele's Laughing Song/ Queen of the Night Aria/ Biassy/ The Musical Snuff-Box/ Like a Bird/ Bell Song/ Serenata Mexicana/ Charmant Oiseau

CD

2006

Documents/Membran 223607-209 (Europe): *Nothing is Bizarre*

    Mein Herr Marquis (Adele's Laughing Song)/ (other songs not by FFJ).

CD

2007

Naxos 8120711F (France): *Florence Foster Jenkins: The Complete Legacy*

    Queen of the Night Aria/ Serenata Mexicana/ The Musical Snuff-Box/ Like a Bird/ Bell Song/ Charmant Oiseau/ Adele's Laughing Song/ Biassy/ Valse Caressante/ (other songs not by FFJ).

[Reissue of 8120711 in different sleeve.]

CD

2012

Klangbad 62LP (Germany): *DJ Marcelle/Another Nice Mess Meets Further Soulmates At Faust Studio Deejay Laboratory*

    The Musical Snuff-Box/ (other songs not by FFJ).

12" LP

2015

World's Worst WWRC001 (Europe): *The World's Worst Records*

    Adele's Laughing Song/ (other songs not by FFJ).

CD

2016

Acrobat ACMCD4388 (UK): *Florence Foster Jenkins*: *The Complete Recordings*

    Queen of the Night/ The Musical Snuff-Box/ Like a Bird/ Bell Song/ Serenata Mexicana/ Charmant Oiseau/ Biassy/ Adele's Laughing Song/ Valse Caressante

CD

Notes

OVERTURE

1. Irving Johnson, 'Discordant Diva's Missing Will', *American Weekly*, 28 January 1945.
2. David Bowie, 'Confessions of a Vinyl Junkie', *Vanity Fair*, November 2003.
3. 'Music: Low, Nagging Earache', *Newsweek,* 30 July 1962.
4. Robert Rushmore, *The Singing Voice,* Dodd Mead, New York, 1971.
5. Milton Bendiner, *Florence Foster Jenkins, An Appreciation*, Melotone Recording Company, New York, 1946.
6. Peter G. Davis, 'The Peculiar Endurance of Opera's Greatest Awful Singer', *New York Magazine,* 28 November 2005.
7. Winthrop Sargeant, 'Soprano's Progress', *Life*, 26 March 1945.
8. *Billboard*, 24 April 1954.
9. William Meredith, *The Hudson Review,* Summer 1955.
10. *PM Daily*, 30 May 1945.
11. Irving Hoffman, 'Tales of Hoffman', *The Hollywood Reporter,* 26 October 1944.
12. Daniel Dixon, 'The Diva of Din', *Coronet*, December 1957.

I WELCOME TO WILKES-BARRE

1. George Brubaker Kulp, *The Luzerne Legal Register*, vol. 12, G.B. Kulp, Wilkes-Barre, 1883.

2. *The History of Luzerne, Lackawanna and Wyoming Counties*, W.W. Munsell & Co, New York, 1880.

3. S.R. Smith, *The Wyoming Valley*, S.R. Smith, Kingston, PA, 1892.

4. Frederick Clifton Pierce, *Foster Genealogy*, W.B. Conkey Company, Chicago, 1899.

5. Mary Jane Hoagland Foster's real age is open to debate. Her memorial in the Foster family mausoleum in the Hollenback cemetery reads that she was ninety years old at the time of her death, which would mean that she was born in 1840 and would have been twenty-four when she married Charles Dorrance Foster. However the Census of 1860 gives her birth date as 1838, the 1870 census as 1845, the 1880 census as 1846, the 1900 census as 1851 and the census of 1910 gives her birth year as 1850, which means that she would have been only eighty when she died and just fourteen when she and Charles married. Neither *Foster Genealogy* (Pierce, 1899) nor *Families of the Wyoming Valley* (Kulp, 1885), nor her obituary in the *New York Times* mention her birth date.

6. Frederick Clifton Pierce, *Foster Genealogy*, W.B. Conkey Company, Chicago, 1899.

7. George B. Kulp, *Families of the Wyoming Valley*, G.B. Kulp, Wilkes-Barre, 1885.

8. 'Death of Hon. C.D. Foster', *Wilkes-Barre Record*, 30 September 1909.

9. *The History of Luzerne, Lackawanna and Wyoming Counties*, W.W. Munsell & Co, New York, 1880.
10. Frederick Clifton Pierce, *Foster Genealogy*, W.B. Conkey Company, Chicago, 1899.
11. H.C. Bradsby, *History of Luzerne County,* S.B. Nelson & Co., Chicago, 1883.
12. George B. Kulp, *Families of the Wyoming Valley,* G.B. Kulp, Wilkes-Barre, 1885.
13. *Wilkes-Barre Record*, 26 July 1881.

2 MRS. DOCTOR JENKINS

1. *Wilkes-Barre Record*, 30 June 1883.
2. *Wilkes-Barre Record*, 22 October 1885.
3. *Wilkes-Barre Record*, 4 February 1888.
4. *Wilkes-Barre Record*, 21 July 1884.
5. Jonathan Grossman, 'The Coal Strike of 1902', *Monthly Labor Review*, October 1975.
6. *The Times* (Philadelphia), 26 June 1887.
7. *New York Press*, 11 January 1903.
8. *The Sun* (New York), 27 November 1944.
9. *Wilkes-Barre Record*, 30 September 1909.

3 THE CURIOUS CASE OF THE MISSING WILL

1. *Pittston Gazette*, 6 October 1909.
2. *Pittston Gazette*, 6 October 1909.
3. *Wilkes-Barre Record*, 9 October 1909.
4. *Wilkes-Barre Record*, 11 December 1909.
5. *Wilkes-Barre Record*, 11 December 1909.
6. *Wilkes-Barre Record*, 11 December 1909.

7. *Wilkes-Barre Record*, 11 December 1909.

8. *Wilkes-Barre Record*, 18 December 1909.

9. *Wilkes-Barre Record*, 9 October 1909.

10. *Indiana Gazette*, 25 October 1910.

4 FLORENCE AND ST. CLAIR

1. Christopher Wren, *Proceedings and Collections of the Wyoming Historical and Geological Society,* WH&GS, 1919.

2. *PM Daily*, 30 May 1945.

3. *New York Daily Tribune,* 24 August 1906.

4. Playbill programme for *A Highland Fling*, 1944.

5. Mozelle Bennett Sawyer, *Joy Fills My Heart*, Traverse City, 1976.

6. Last Will and Testament of Charles Dorrance Foster (signed November 1903, updated January 1909).

7. *PM Daily*, 30 May 1945.

8. *PM Daily*, 30 May 1945.

9. *New York Herald*, 30 July 1916.

10. Kate Louise Roberts, *The Club Woman's Handybook of Programs and Club Management*, Funk and Wagnalls, New York 1914.

5 FLO'S A SINGER

1. Daniel Dixon, 'The Diva of Din', *Coronet*, December 1957.

2. *New York Herald*, 21 May 1911.

3. *New York Herald*, 16 May 1915.

4. *New York Herald*, 2 January 1916.

5. 'Charles Cameron Bell in Demand', *Musical Courier*, 3 August 1916.

6. *New York Herald*, 28 November 1917.

7. *Musical Courier*, 12 February 1920.

8. *Musical Courier*, 22 April 1920.

9. *Musical Courier*, 2 June 1921.

10. *The Sun* (New York), 21 April 1918.

11. *Musical Courier*, 23 November 1922.

12. Mozelle Bennett Sawyer, *Joy Fills My Heart* , Traverse City, 1976.

13. *Amsterdam (NY) Evening Recorder*, 20 October 1923.

14. *American Cloak and Suit Review*, 1921.

15. 'Women to Manage new Beethoven Orchestra', *The Sun* (New York), 6 October 1927.

6 I HOPE THE BOAT SINKS!

1. Claude Henry Neuffer, *Names in South Carolina*, University of South Carolina, 1972.

2. Daniel Dixon, 'The Diva of Din', *Coronet*, December 1957.

3. 'The Society Songbird Who Sprouts Wings Once a Year', *Milwaukee Sentinel*, 6 February 1944.

4. Milton Bendiner, *Florence Foster Jenkins, An Appreciation*, Melotone Recording Company, 1946.

5. *Philadelphia Enquirer*, 11 August 1943.

7 MEET MR. MCMOON

1. *PM Daily*, 30 May 1945.

2. Richard S. Davis, 'Journal Music Critic Reports on Funniest, Saddest of all Concerts', *Milwaukee Journal*, 27 October 1944.

3. 'Dead Cool: Florence Foster Jenkins', *Daily Beast*, 10 July 2010.

4. Paul Moor, 'Roses For Lady Florence', *Harper's Magazine*, 1963.

5. Original sleeve notes to *A Florence! Foster!! Jenkins!!! Recital!!!!*, RCA, 1954.

6. Original sleeve notes to *A Florence! Foster!! Jenkins!!! Recital!!!!*, RCA, 1954.

7. *San Antonio Evening News,* 8 April 1922.

8. The Hungerford Tape, 1970 (see Chapter 10, note 11).

9. The Hungerford Tape, 1970 (see Chapter 10, note 11).

10. *New York Times*, 3 January 1939.

11. Paul Moor, 'Roses For Lady Florence', *Harper's Magazine*, 1963.

12. *The Musician: America's Leading Magazine for Musicians, Music-lovers, Teachers and Students*, vols 44-45, N. Jaakobs, 1939.

13. *The Musician: America's Leading Magazine for Musicians, Music-lovers, Teachers and Students*, vols 44-45, N. Jaakobs, 1939.

14. *Musical Courier*, 15 October 1942.

15. *Musical Courier*, 23 November 1922.

16. *Musical Courier*, 23 November 1922.

17. Mozelle Bennett Sawyer, *Joy Fills My Heart*, Traverse City, 1976.

18. Richard S. Davis, 'Journal Music Critic Reports on Funniest, Saddest of all Concerts', *Milwaukee Journal*, 27 October 1944.

8 MADAME MAKES A RECORD

1. Milton Bendiner, *Florence Foster Jenkins, An Appreciation*, Melotone Recording Company, 1946.
2. Milton Bendiner, *Florence Foster Jenkins, An Appreciation*, Melotone Recording Company, 1946.
3. Vernon Alfred Howard, *Charm and Speed: Virtuosity in the Performing Arts*, Peter Lang Publishing, 2008.
4. 'Music: Recital Mill', *Time*, 2 November 1942.
5. Milton Bendiner, *Florence Foster Jenkins, An Appreciation*, Melotone Recording Company, 1946.
6. *Washington Post*, 19 December 2014.
7. Recalled by Adolf Pollitz on the Hungerford Tape, 1970.
8. Paul Moor, 'Roses For Lady Florence', *Harper's Magazine*, 1963.

9 LIVE AT CARNEGIE HALL

1. Richard S. Davis, 'Journal Music Critic Reports on Funniest, Saddest of all Concerts', *Milwaukee Journal*, 27 October 1944.
2. Clipping dated 9 November 1935, held in the Florence Foster Jenkins Scrapbook, New York Public Library (presumably from the *Musical Courier*).
3. 'Worst Record of the Year Claimed by Maker of Disks', *Spokane Daily Chronicle*, 12 April 1954.
4. *New York Daily Mirror*, 5 November 1943.
5. *New York Post*, 17 November 1944.
6. Paul Moor, 'Roses For Lady Florence', *Harper's Magazine*, 1963.
7. *The Musician: America's Leading Magazine for Musicians,*

    Music-lovers, Teachers and Students, vols 44-45, N. Jaakobs, 1939.

8. *New York Times*, 24 October 1944.

9. 'Music: Recital Mill', *Time*, 2 November 1942.

10. *New York Post*, 6 November 1944.

11. *New York Post*, 26 October 1944.

12. Richard S. Davis, 'Journal Music Critic Reports on Funniest, Saddest of all Concerts', *Milwaukee Journal*, 27 October 1944.

13. *San Bernardino County Sun*, 26 April 1981.

14. *New York Post*, 26 October 1944.

15. Brooks Peters, 'Florence Nightingale', *Opera News*, June 2001.

16. Richard S. Davis, 'Journal Music Critic Reports on Funniest, Saddest of all Concerts', *Milwaukee Journal*, 27 October 1944.

17. *PM Daily*, 26 October 26 1944.

18. *Los Angeles Times*, 29 October 1944.

19. Richard S. Davis, 'Journal Music Critic Reports on Funniest, Saddest of all Concerts', *Milwaukee Journal*, 27 October 1944.

20. Milton Bendiner, *Florence Foster Jenkins, An Appreciation*, Melotone Recording Company, 1946.

10 GOODBYE

1. *Times Herald* (New York), 3 November 1944.

2. *Opera News*, March 1963.

3. 'The Society Songbird Who Sprouts Wings Once a Year', *American Weekly*, 6 February 1944.

4. *Sunday Times* (Perth), 2 April 1944.

5. *Time*, 4 December 1944.

6. 'Famed Woman Musician Dies', *Wilkes-Barre Record*, 30 November 1944.

7. 'Famed Woman Musician Dies', *Wilkes-Barre Record*, 30 November 1944.

8. *New York World-Telegram*, 26 October 1944.

9. Irving Johnson, 'Discordant Diva's Missing Will', *American Weekly*, 28 January 1945.

10. Irving Johnson, 'Discordant Diva's Missing Will', *American Weekly*, 28 January 1945.

11. The Hungerford Tape, as it is known in FFJ circles, was recorded by pianist Bruce Hungerford in 1970 and is an audio verité recording featuring Kathleen Bayfield, Florence Darnault, Bruce Hungerford, Adolf Pollitz and, possibly, others (there appears to be at least one other voice on the tape). Although often cited as an important source of information – it includes sections read from St. Clair Bayfield's unfinished biography of Florence and is the only source for the suggestion that Florence caught syphilis from Frank Jenkins – it is highly inaccurate and cannot be entirely trusted. Whether this is due to Florence's 'reinterpretation' of her life story, to Kay Bayfield's obvious dislike of her, or to the passing of years and the fading memories of the participants cannot be known.

FINALE

1. Irving Kolodin, 'New York Round-Up', *Ottawa Citizen*, 24 April 1954.

2. *Life*, 25 May 1962.

3. Patricia Volk, *The Art of Being a Woman: My Mother, Schiaparelli, and Me,* Random House, 2013.

4. Bruno Costemalle, *Mais où est Passé le Crâne de Mozart?,* Editions du Panama, 2007.

5. *Guardian*, 3 November 2005.

6. The Empire Film Podcast, May 2015.

7. David Bowie, 'Confessions of a Vinyl Junkie', *Vanity Fair*, November 2003.

8. *Washington Post,* 12 March 1976.

9. Mozelle Bennett Sawyer, *Joy Fills My Heart*, Traverse City, 1976.

10. *PM Daily*, 30 May 1945.

Acknowledgements

None of this would have been possible without the sterling efforts shown by other writers and researchers over the seventy-plus years since Florence Foster Jenkins passed away, but special credit must go to Donald Collup and Gregor Benko whose documentary *Florence Foster Jenkins: A World of Her Own* is a must-watch for anyone interested in her story. Gregor Benko has been especially helpful, correcting my mistakes and helping point the way when I strayed off path: this book would be nothing without his (and his family's) patience and kindness.

My thanks to Nancy Elston Schimmel, Florence's cousin, for her genuine warmth, help and encouragement; to Peter Quilter, the author of *Glorious!* and Stephen Temperley, the author of *Souvenir, a Fantasia on the Life of Florence Foster Jenkins;* thanks to Richard Connema and to Mark McMunn, Cosme's nephew, all of whom gave generously of their time to help with this book. Thank you too to Alexandra M. Griffiths of the Interlibrary & Document Services of the New York Public Library for her invaluable help and patience, and to Joseph Levy for his time and assistance in transcribing the St. Clair Bayfield diaries. Huge thanks to Nikki Griffiths and David Marshall at Duckworth Overlook for their faith in this project, and to Deborah Blake, my editor, for making sense of all of this.

Special thanks to my husband, Niall, for his unending support and belief.

Index